The ASSIST Program

Affective/Social Skills: Instructional Strategies and Techniques

Teaching Friendship Skills: Primary Version

A Validated Washington State Innovative Education Program

This version of *Teaching Friendship Skills*
is a product of the joint efforts of

Pat Huggins
Larry Moen
and
Donna Wood Manion

ISBN #0-944584-69-1

Published & Distributed by:

SOPRIS WEST, INC.
1140 Boston Avenue • Longmont, Colorado 80501 • (303) 651-2829

Table of Contents

Students will discuss what they think are the most important characteristics of a friend.

Students will nominate class members who exhibit friendly behaviors.

Students will learn behaviors that prevent the development of friendships by identifying behaviors they dislike in others.

Students will identify behaviors they have that interfere with friendships.

Students will learn some reasons behind put-down behavior, as well as the fact that giving put-downs can cause others not to trust them.

Students will learn techniques to help them change their put-down behaviors.

Students will learn specific behaviors that promote friendship.

Students will practice specific behaviors that promote friendship.

Students will evaluate their own friendship behavior and devise an action plan for improvement.

Overview of the ASSIST Program
Affective/**S**ocial **S**kills: **I**nstructional **S**trategies and **T**echniques

ASSIST is an affective education program designed to increase students' growth in the areas of self-concept, self-management, interpersonal relationships, and emotional understanding. ASSIST manuals provide a complete guide for elementary teachers to actively involve students in developing critical personal/social skills. The ASSIST Program can be incorporated into an existing program or it can stand alone as a curriculum for personal growth and interpersonal relations.

The ASSIST curriculum is the result of an extensive review of child development theory and research, a review of existing social/emotional education programs, and the contributions of many teachers and students who participated in the development of the Program. **ASSIST incorporates concepts and procedures from social learning theory, behavioristic and humanistic psychology, and from proven educational practices.** The curriculum involves students in a series of cognitively-oriented lessons and experiential learning activities.

The ASSIST lessons include:

- A "To the Teacher" section which provides a theoretical background for lesson concepts;

- A "scripted" lesson that includes everything necessary to teach lesson concepts and skills;

- A series of transparency masters and handouts (student worksheets); and

- A variety of "Supplementary Activities" designed to integrate the lessons into basic subject areas.

ASSIST was developed with Title IV-C Innovative Education Funds and was evaluated in second through sixth grade classrooms in four school districts. **Statistically significant gains in self-concept and social skills occurred in eight out of nine assessments.** As a result, ASSIST was validated in Washington State and designated cost-effective and exportable. It is now in the State's "Bank of Proven Practices," a clearinghouse for quality programs.

The ASSIST manuals currently in print include the following:

- *Building Self-Esteem in the Classroom*—This manual includes a series of sequential lessons and activities designed to promote self-awareness. Students learn that they have a unique combination of intelligences, skills, and abilities and learn how to identify their particular strengths. They learn to focus on their strengths and use them as springboards for new successes. They learn to use the techniques of positive inner speech to build self-esteem and to cope effectively with mistakes and put-downs. Also included in the manual are workbooks for both primary and intermediate students and a self-esteem unit for middle school students.

- *Teaching About Sexual Abuse*—The lessons in this manual are designed to provide students with information about sexual abuse in a low-key, matter-of-fact way. Lessons focus on: (1) children's right to reject inappropriate behavior; (2) assertiveness skills helpful in the prevention of sexual abuse; and (3) establishing family and community support systems.

- *Teaching Cooperation Skills*—This manual includes a series of lessons and experiential activities designed to teach students the skills necessary for cooperative learning to take place. Lessons focus on the skills of self-management, listening, and collaborative problem solving. Students learn to resolve conflicts through negotiation and compromise. A wide variety of cooperative learning activities are included so that these skills can be applied and practiced.

- *Creating A Caring Classroom*—This manual includes a collection of strategies designed to promote mutual respect, trust, risk-taking, and support in the classroom. Included are: (1) getting acquainted activities; (2) classroom management procedures; (3) an affective behavior scale and behavior improvement strategies for students with special needs; (4) a relaxation training program; and (5) a large collection of activities for building a cohesive and caring classroom community.

- *Helping Kids Handle Anger*—This manual includes lessons designed to enable students to acknowledge, accept, and constructively express anger. Students learn: (1) to use inner speech to inhibit aggressive behaviors; (2) to use thinking skills for choosing constructive behaviors when angry; (3) appropriate language to express anger; (4) a variety of techniques to release energy after anger arousal; and (5) ways to deal with the anger of others. Role-play and puppets are utilized to encourage active and creative student involvement.

Introduction

This curriculum provides teachers and school counselors with systematic procedures for enhancing social competence in elementary-age children. The purpose of the lessons and activities in this program is two-fold: (1) to help students learn the key relational skills which will enable them to initiate and maintain friendships, and (2) to improve the social climate within the classroom so that interpersonal problems do not disrupt academic learning. Each lesson introduces specific friendship skills that have been shown to increase peer acceptance and enhance students' ability to interact positively with all their classmates.

The lessons are based on current learning theory and have been field-tested in elementary classrooms. Much of the instructional approach is similar to the teaching of basic academic competencies. In addition to direct cognitive instruction, affective and behavioral components are also used. Each lesson includes a sequence of motivation, practice, and maintenance activities. Students are:

1. Involved in group discussions regarding friendship behaviors, issues, and problems;

2. Given opportunities to see friendship skills modeled;

3. Involved in role-play and other structured activities which allow them to practice the skills;

4. Given feedback regarding their practice; and

5. Provided with structures for integrating friendship skills into their daily lives through goal setting and reinforcement (maintenance and transfer of training).

The lessons in this manual bring the fundamental issues of friendship to students' awareness. Students are given opportunities to discover what the ingredients of a relationship are and what makes it a friendship. They engage in activities to discover similarities and positive qualities in their classmates, both of which are prerequisites to friendship. Students determine how **they** want to be treated by those they consider friends. They then take a close look at their own behavior and set appropriate goals for change. Finally, they learn ways to give authentic praise and help to one another.

Why teach friendship skills in the classroom?

Teachers are well aware of how disruptive interpersonal problems can be in a classroom. Often, considerable time is spent soothing students who are upset because no one will play with them, trying to protect students who are constantly harassed by other class members, encouraging shy students to try to make friends, and dealing with students who are trying to enhance their social status through attention-getting misbehavior. Many teachers have concluded that the time spent trying to cope with students' social deficits could be better spent in teaching students how to get along with others. In so doing they have confirmed the research which shows that friendship skills can be learned. They've also found that direct instruction in friendship-making techniques makes a positive change in classroom climate.

Problems in the classroom related to social immaturity or a lack of friendship skills seem to be on the rise. There are many reasons for this, but the leading cause is that our social institutions are undergoing great changes. Due to the "meltdown" of the nuclear family, more and more students are being raised in high-risk environments where they are not learning basic social skills. Our mobile society also contributes to disruption in socialization. On the average, the American family moves about once every four years. This presents more challenges to students in friendship-making than in the past. Teachers often overestimate how well students know each other or how comfortable they feel with each other. In fact, many students today do not feel a sense of psychological security or safety with their classmates. While teachers cannot take on the responsibility for a child's needs that parenting requires, they can take some steps to ensure that their classroom is a place where every student feels accepted by at least a few of his or her peers.

Friendship skill deficits do more than lead to class disruptions or to isolated or rejected children. Research evidence over the past several years indicates that there is a direct correlation between friendship patterns and academic performance.

> *Although educators generally have not considered student friendships relevant to individual students' cognitive development, our research evidence and experience indicate that they are related. In fact, friendships classmates have for one another, along with their willingness to help and support one another, represent important ingredients for the enhancement of individual academic achievement .... Strong relationships with others are not only valuable in themselves; they also enhance cognitive development in the classroom.*

> Richard Schmuck and Pat Schmuck (1974)
> *Group Processes in the Classroom*

Children who feel they do not belong often find it difficult to focus on academic tasks.

> *Positive interpersonal relations among students are necessary both for problem solving in groups and for general classroom enjoyment of instructional activity. The psychological security and safety necessary for open exploration of instructional tasks is based upon feelings of being accepted, liked, and supported by fellow students.*

> David Johnson and Roger Johnson (1975)
> *Learning Together and Alone*

Even though some students are able to master academics without experiencing successful peer relationships, academic achievement alone does not prepare a child for a successful life. Friendships are central to the quality of children's lives. Even the presence of nurturing adults cannot alleviate the loneliness children experience when they lack a friend. Children need the confirmation of a peer who is not a family member. Feelings of being accepted socially, of being liked for oneself and for one's own actions and behaviors, are extremely important to the development of emotional security. The inability to make friends erodes a child's self-esteem. Since so many of the problems and joys we experience at each stage in life are interpersonal in nature, teaching friendship skills is a gift we can give to students which will benefit them throughout their lives.

What are the factors that contribute to children's friendship-making?

There are many factors over which a child has little or no control which are likely to affect the way the child is viewed by peers and which influence how easily the child makes friends. Physical appearance, intellectual abilities, family background, and even athletic prowess may influence a child's social status during elementary-school years. Along with these aspects of natural attractiveness, a child's outgoingness toward others is also a strong factor in social attraction.

Sometimes natural endowments present a child with a difficult path to friendship-making. Life events may add to this difficulty. A child may have had poor models and a lack of reinforcement or opportunity for positive social behavior. When these natural forces do not work to help a child find success in peer relationships, a child can benefit from adult help in mastering the skills of friendship. Research over the past ten years has shown that teaching social responses to help improve a child's social interactions can help compensate for limitations which have affected a child's friendship-making abilities.

It should be understood that the objective of social skills instruction is not to create "popular" children, but to help children, whatever their personality styles or life history, to develop positive relationships with at least one or two of their peers.

What are the key skills for friendship-making?

A number of studies have indicated that children tend to like children who have helped them. Additional studies show that to gain acceptance from peers, children must be able to seek out others and be agreeable to them when asked to do something reasonable. Children who give others a large number of positive responses are much more likely to be chosen as friends.

Communication and listening skills are also important. Children who are poor communicators or listeners are more likely to be rejected or ignored. Children skilled in initiating conversations have more friends. Excessive shyness or not knowing how to make positive approaches toward other children will inhibit development of friendship.

The ability to control aggression is also a key skill in social attractiveness. Disrupting the activities of other children or initiating unprovoked physical attacks are major factors in being disliked.

The lessons in this manual are designed to address each of these skill areas. The ASSIST manual *Helping Kids Handle Anger* provides more comprehensive skill training in managing aggression. Conflict resolution, negotiation, and compromise are also key skills. These will be addressed in the forthcoming ASSIST manual, *Solving Friendship Problems*.

How to Use This Curriculum

Lesson Grade Levels

Each lesson in this curriculum presents one or more concepts that are central to social functioning. Because of the timelessness and generality of most of these concepts, the same lessons can be taught to students as they advance through the grades. Each time students are exposed to the concepts in a lesson, they are able to consider them from a new frame of reference and make new and more precise applications. Following each of the lessons, there are specific supplementary activities recommended for 1st, 2nd, and 3rd graders. Lessons and supplementary activities for 4th, 5th, and 6th graders are found in the ASSIST manual *Teaching Friendship Skills: Intermediate Version.*

Lesson Overview

Each lesson has a clearly stated objective, a list of all the materials needed to teach the lesson, and a "To the Teacher" section. This section outlines the planning necessary for the lesson. It provides theoretical background on the concepts presented. It also includes a summary of the skills taught in the lesson, the methods used, and suggestions for effective teaching.

Lesson Presentation Section

The "Lesson Presentation" section gives step-by-step instructions on how to conduct the lesson. A "scripted" presentation, provided in boldface type, is included to put the "meat on the bones" of the lesson. It provides a model for everything that needs to be said to impart lesson concepts. However, this is simply a model; you will want to rephrase the script, saying things in your own words to accommodate aspects of your particular students' frame of reference. The success of the lesson will depend on your ability to provide examples and illustrations of lesson concepts that your students will relate to. It will also depend on your sense of how to pace the lesson, expanding or shortening sections to fit your students' needs. All this implies that you will need to be very familiar with a lesson before you teach it. One way to gain this familiarity is by taping a lesson and listening to it as you travel to and from school. Or you can order tapes of these lessons from the publisher of this manual. Becoming familiar with the lessons in this way will enable you to "ad lib" the lesson, which frees you to more easily handle the many lesson transparencies.

Lessons conclude with a debriefing section and techniques to facilitate generalization and transfer of training to real life situations.

Transparencies

Each lesson includes a series of transparency masters for students whose learning style says, "Don't just tell me, show me!"

Handouts

Reproducible student handouts/worksheets also accompany each lesson. These worksheets give students an opportunity to process lesson concepts as well as to demonstrate that they were "attending and receiving" during the lesson presentation and discussion.

Supplementary Activities

Following each lesson are a number of "Supplementary Activities" designed to appeal to students of varying abilities. These are designed to help students "process" the ideas presented in the lesson and to provide opportunities for them to practice the personal/social skills related to the lesson concepts. These activities allow for integration of the lesson concepts and help nudge students into higher levels of social reasoning. Many of these activities relate to basic subject areas in the regular curriculum.

The Appendices: Other Resources for Promoting Friendship Skills

- **Using Literature to Enhance Students' Understanding of Friendship**

  An extensive list of children's books relating to friendship themes is provided. Reading some of these books to your class or setting up a "Friendship Reading Center" is a wonderful way to promote knowledge and discussion of friendship issues.

- **Friendship Games**

  The games provided in this manual have been tried in many classroom situations and have been found to have high student appeal. They naturally and enjoyably reinforce the concepts presented in the lessons.

- **School-Wide Procedures That Promote Friendship**

  Many schools like to devote a particular week or month to focus on the theme of friendship. This section provides ideas and materials to implement such a plan.

- **Posters**

  The posters included in this section can be hung permanently in the classroom and at other places in the school building to remind students of friendship behaviors.

Scheduling the Lessons

Some teachers integrate these lessons into their health, social studies, and language arts/communication curricula. Others set up a formal "social skills" period and teach lessons once per week, or use a "unit" format, teaching a lesson or doing an activity on a daily basis for a period of time. Some teachers prefer to introduce this material more casually, teaching a lesson from time to time when they see a need for instruction in a specific skill presented in a lesson.

Lessons should last 30 to 45 minutes, depending on students' attention span. Some lessons can be divided and taught in segments.

It is helpful to support the learning and goals generated by the lessons with reminders and suggestions throughout the school day and week. Teaching the lesson early in the school day enables you to capitalize on opportunities during the remainder of the day to use lesson vocabulary and encourage students to apply the skills that were introduced that morning.

Using the Techniques of Role-Play and Group Discussion to Teach Friendship Skills

- **Role-Play**

  Role-play provides students with an opportunity to practice using the friendship skills presented in the lessons. Discussing friendship behaviors helps students learn to talk about friendship skills. Role-play helps students learn to enact these skills. A unique advantage of role-play is the opportunity to practice new ways of behaving. A shy student may practice initiating a conversation through role-playing. As a result of the role-play experience, this student may be able to incorporate a new behavior into his or her daily life.

  By putting themselves in the place of others, students become sensitive to others' feelings. Because role-playing is as close as we can come to actually being another person, it strongly encourages the development of empathy. For example, by playing the role of a scapegoat, a bully may understand how it feels to be picked on. A scapegoat playing a bully may begin to see why his or her behavior attracts a bully. Both can see what some alternative actions are.

  Role-play involves: (1) the discussion and analysis of social situations; (2) an original enactment; (3) discussion of the observers' reaction to the enactment; (4) exploration of alternatives through further role-playing; and (5) drawing conclusions or making generalizations regarding social situations.

  The following are some suggestions on ways to make role-play more effective:

  - Wait until the class members are acquainted and at ease with one another before you introduce role-playing.

  - Anticipate some self-consciousness on the part of students.

  - Set rules to curtail acting silly or aggressive behavior during role-play.

– Help students feel at ease by making clear to them that this is not a performance and that they will not be judged on how well they can act.

– Explain that the purpose of the role-plays is to test ideas to see if certain solutions to problem situations really work.

– Keep a nonjudgmental attitude. Be warm and responsive to what students do and say.

– Choose role-play situations that are relevant to students' lives.

– Make sure both observers and players fully understand the role-play situation before it is enacted.

– Try to create a positive classroom environment by explaining that students should not judge one another and that there is not necessarily one right solution to a role-play situation.

– Invite students to volunteer to role-play only after they have thought of a possible solution to the role-play situation.

– Players should be able to describe their characters, the scene, and the setting in detail before they begin the role-play. Help them by asking questions such as, "Where are you?" and "What are you doing?"

– Ask students to try to feel, act, and talk like the person they are role-playing. They should try to forget that they are being observed.

– Observers should be as quiet and unobtrusive as possible. They should act as if they were hidden cameras watching the action but not interfering with it in any way, especially not through criticizing the players.

– Give observers the task of silently asking themselves questions like, "What would I do in this situation?" or "Is there another way to solve the problem?" as they watch the role-play.

– Once a role-play begins, address players by their role name, not their real name. This helps them stay in character throughout the scene.

– If students block on what to say, you can either use stage whispers to coach them or stop the action to brainstorm with the observers what could be said or done next. Resume the action as quickly as possible.

– If appropriate to the learning intended from the role, interject questions to the characters as the action unfolds. Questions about what the character might be feeling are particularly helpful.

– Keep each role-play to a maximum of five minutes.

– Debrief the role-play by exploring feelings the student had toward the character he or she played and toward the other characters involved. Make clear by your questions that students and roles are separate. When concluded, thank students by their real names.

– During the discussion of the role-play, emphasize that alternative solutions are possible.

– The same role-play situation can be enacted again with different players who may demonstrate other approaches to the problem.

– Encourage students to generalize the role-play to their own lives by asking them to think about questions such as, "Has a situation like this ever happened to you?" or "Does this situation remind you of something in your own life?"

- **Group Discussion**

Group discussion is a valuable teaching tool, especially when the discussion is structured so that students who are functioning on a high social level can share their knowledge, experience, and opinions with their peers. Studies have shown that, even at the kindergarten level, students are influenced more by the comments of peers than by the comments of their teacher. Thus, at times when you want students to function on a higher social level it is more productive to expose them to comments of socially mature peers who are discussing appropriate social behavior than for you to talk about this behavior.

The following are some suggestions to make group discussion more effective:

– If possible, use a place in your classroom where students can sit in a circle so they can all see each other.

– Set some basic rules regarding group discussion at the beginning of the first lesson. Some suggested rules are:

  1. Students must raise hands if they want to speak;

  2. When someone is speaking everyone else must look at them and listen quietly; and

  3. Students should not mention names when relating stories. Instead they should say, "Someone I know . . . ."

– At the beginning of each lesson, tell students you will be calling on them frequently during the discussion.

– Ask open-ended questions such as, "What can you tell us about . . . ?" or "Can you tell us more about . . . ?"

– When you call on a student and he or she doesn't answer immediately, be sure to allow sufficient "wait time" (perhaps five seconds) before going on.

– Don't force shy students to participate. Explain that "pass" is an acceptable answer, after they have thought about a question. You can, at times, include shy students by asking questions that can be answered with one word or a nod.

– If a student who is not attending well is not ready to give a response to a question, say you will come back to him or her shortly for the response.

– If a student is dominating the discussion, say something like, "We have to move on, but I would be interested in hearing more later."

– Use the technique of "thumbs up or down" to get all students' responses to general questions.

– Increase students' opportunity for participation in the discussion by arranging for them to have "Learning Partners" or small groups to discuss topics with.

– Don't ask questions and then answer them yourself.

– Don't rephrase students' responses to make them more acceptable to you.

– Don't repeat a question after calling on a student. This trains students not to listen.

– Don't repeat students' answers. This prevents students from responding directly to each other and encourages students to give less complete answers, since they know you will modify their response in an acceptable manner.

– **Discuss** ideas presented in the lesson with students; avoid giving "sermonettes."

– Whenever possible, structure the discussion to encourage students with high social functioning to suggest examples of the concepts you want to get across.

Suggestions for Enhancing the Teaching of This Curriculum

• Emphasize the fun activities that accompany each lesson.

• Supply students with a "think pad" to write on during lessons.

• Make sure students keep all handouts and materials from the lessons in their "Friendship Folders."

• Let students' interests, responses, needs, and contributions shape the lessons rather than trying to complete a lesson in a given time.

• Incorporate the vocabulary lists and writing activities in the lessons into your language arts program.

• Use the art ideas as part of your art program.

Classroom Procedures That Can Aid in the Development of Friendships Within the Classroom

In addition to the lessons presented in this manual, there are some strategies which can be used throughout the school day to enable students to practice the friendship skills you have taught them and which will establish a more positive social climate in your classroom. The most powerful strategy you can use is cooperative learning. See the ASSIST manual *Teaching Cooperation Skills* for lessons on how to teach your students the prerequisite skills for working cooperatively on academic tasks.

Once you are using a cooperative learning structure, regroup frequently. Frequent regrouping is helpful because: (1) it places students in close personal contact with students they normally do not interact with. This helps initiate new friendships; (2) it provides more opportunities for isolates to interact with other students; (3) it can help prevent the formation of cliques; (4) it can provide opportunities for unpopular students to be "discovered" or to show skills or attractive traits they may have that would otherwise go unnoticed because no one interacts with them; and (5) it provides all students an opportunity to have contact with those socially competent students who can provide models for developing friendship skills.

Both random regrouping and sociometric regrouping are effective ways to make sure all students have maximum opportunity to interact with each other. In sociometric grouping you can identify students who have friendship problems and carefully place them in groups where they have an opportunity to work with potential friends. Random regrouping is beneficial because it: (1) provides a means by which groups accept unpopular classmates (they know groups will be of short existence); (2) avoids student pressure for inclusion of friends; (3) reduces students' fear of being chosen last; and (4) allows a group to be formed quickly.

Grouping students randomly or sociometrically creates opportunities for students to make friends because **proximity** is one of the antecedents of friendship. The more often students interact, the more likely they are to become friends.

The Development of Children's Understanding of Friendship

- **Developmental Stages**

  Developmental psychologist Robert Selman of Harvard has found that children go through a series of four stages of friendship development. These stages evolve from an initial preoccupation with self, or viewing friendship in an egocentric way, to the ability to see the perspective of others, or to empathize. The following is a brief description of each of these four stages:

  Stage 1 (ages four to nine): At this stage children do not understand that dealing with others involves give and take. A "good" friendship is one in which one person does what the other person wants. If one child says, "Let's ride bikes," and the other says, "I don't want to," a normal response from a Stage 1 child would be, "Then you're not my friend."

- **Stage 2 (ages six to twelve):** Children have the ability to see that friendship doesn't work unless both friends meet each other's needs. "He does things I like, and I do things he likes." This is the stage of two-way "fairweather" friendship. The child still sees the basic purpose of friendship as serving self-interest, rather than mutual interests. "He likes me and I like him. We do things for each other."

- **Stage 3 (ages nine to fifteen):** It is in the transition from Stage 2 to Stage 3, typically in late childhood, that children begin to consider the other person's point of view. They begin thinking about mutual commitment and loyalty in a friendship, rather than "What should I do to get what I want?" The thought often is, "What should I do to make my friend happy?" In this stage, friends share more than secrets, agreements, or plans; they share feelings and personal problems. "She is my best friend. We can tell each other things we can't tell anyone else. We stick with each other through thick and thin." The limitation of this stage is that friendships are often exclusive and possessive, with jealousies being common.

- **Stage 4 (ages twelve and older):** After children finish the stage where friendships are so possessive, they move to a stage where friends can be close, yet grant each other the freedom to develop other relationships. "If you are really close friends you have to trust and support each other. We have to let each other have other friends, too."

These progressions in social understanding are made possible, in part, by parallel progressions from concrete to abstract reasoning in a child's intellectual development. Generally, primary age students are in Stages 1 and 2 of social reasoning. In the intermediate grades, students move into Stages 2 and 3. However, this development of social understanding depends on both growing intellectual skills and on specific social experiences. Since these vary widely among individuals, in a given classroom it is possible to have students in many stages of social reasoning.

- **Empathy**

The stages of social awareness which have been outlined by Selman also represent the base for empathy. Young children don't naturally see things from another's point of view. As children reach middle childhood, they become increasingly more facile in cognitive skills and gain in the ability to empathize. Development of empathy, however, depends on experience as well as cognitive capacity.

Elements of empathy are eminently teachable to children of all school ages. The ability to understand what someone else thinks or feels is not an all-or-none phenomenon, but has a gradual and variable development. The younger child will begin by appreciating new perspectives most similar to his or her own. Training in empathy involves providing relevant social experiences and examining them in an educational way. It is thought to occur through exposure to reasoning at one stage above the stage that the student is using. Students will have excellent opportunities to hear the various social reasoning stages of their classmates as they discuss concepts, questions, and role-plays represented in the lessons in this manual.

Suggested Readings on Children's Friendships

Arrezo, D. & Stocking, H. (1975). *Helping friendless children: A guide for teachers and parents*. Boys Town, NE: Boys Town Center for the Study of Youth Development.

Asher, S. & Gottman, J. (Eds.). (1981). *The development of children's friendships*. Cambridge, MA: Cambridge University Press.

Cottman, J. & Conso, J. (1975). Social interaction, social competence, and friendship in children. *Child Development, 46*, 709-718.

Damon, W. (1977). *The social world of the child*. San Francisco: Jossey-Bass.

Flavell, J. (1974). The development of inference about others. In T. Mischel (Ed.), *Understanding other persons*. Oxford, England: Blackwell.

Foot, H.C., Chapman, A.J., & Smith, J.R. (Eds.). (in press). *Friendship and childhood relations*. London, England: Wiley.

Fox, C.L. & LaVine Weaver, F. (1983). *Unlocking doors to friendship*. Rolling Hills Estates, CA: B.L. Winch & Assoc.

Hartup, W. (1988). Conflict and the friendship relations of young children. *Child Development, 9*(6), 1490-1600.

Hayes, D. (1978). Cognitive bases for liking and disliking among school children. *Child Development, 49*, 906-909.

Oden, S. & Asher, S. (1977). Coaching children in social skills and friendships making. *Child Development, 48*, 495-506.

Rubin, A. (1980). *Children's friendships*. Cambridge, MA: Harvard University Press.

Selman, R. (1981). The child as a friendship philosopher. In S. Asher & J. Gottman (Eds.), *The development of children's friendships*. Cambridge, MA: Cambridge University Press.

Staub, E. (1971). Use of role-playing and induction in training for pro-social behavior. *Child Development, 42*, 805-816.

Vorenhorst, B. (1983). *Real friends: Becoming the friend you'd like to have*. New York: Harper & Row.

Youniss, J. & Volpe J. (1978). A relational analysis of children's friendship. In W. Damon (Ed.), *Social cognition*. San Francisco: Jossey-Bass.

Behaviors That Help Kids Have Friends

Objective

Students will discuss what they think are the most important characteristics of a friend.

Students will nominate class members who exhibit friendly behaviors.

Materials

Blank transparency and pen

Transparency #1 - "What We Want Most in a Friend"

Transparencies #2A and #2B - "What We Want Most in a Friend—Words" (cut into pieces)

Handout #1 - "What I Want Most in a Friend"

Handout #2 - "Friendship Word List"

Handout #3 - "Kids in Our Class Who Have Friendly Behaviors"

Poster - "Tally Sheet: Results of the Friendship Survey"

"Friendship Folder" for each student (can be a large piece of construction paper)

Pencil, markers, and crayons

To the Teacher

This lesson is an orientation to the concept that there are certain behaviors that cause others to want to choose us as friends. Students are asked to think about what they would like in an ideal friend. Then an attempt is made to subtly lead them to an awareness of what they need to be like themselves in order to have friends. This approach avoids lecturing or sermonizing. Students learn that although having friends may be a talent, it is also something that can be learned. The lesson emphasizes that having a friend is within every one's grasp providing he or she is willing to work at prosocial behaviors.

In this lesson students have an opportunity to vote as a group on what they value in a friend and to decide individually what is important to them in a friend. Students also nominate their classmates on a friendship behavior survey.

Tally the survey as soon as possible after the lesson and share the results with the class (Poster) and/or place it on a bulletin board. Survey results can also be shared with parents of students selected. (These students are likely to be students with high interpersonal I.Q.s). It's not important that all students are selected in the survey, as the purpose of it is to point out students who are class role models of friendly behavior. This tends to reinforce prosocial behavior in others.

See the suggested list of picture books and read-aloud books in Appendix A. You may want to set up a "Friendship Reading Center" in your room including some of these books.

Along with the books, the "Friendship Word List" (Handout #2) can be easily integrated into a whole language program. The words can be used for spelling, vocabulary study, or creating a story.

Students should also be given folders or construction paper so they can make a "Friendship Folder." Students should keep all handouts you give them during this unit in this folder.

At the end of the lesson, students are asked to write a friendship behavior in the middle of their hand that they are going to work on. To facilitate transfer of training, remind students at the beginning and end of each day for the next few days to try to find an opportunity to do the behavior they selected.

The Supplementary Activities that follow the lesson can be used to extend the learning and provide more practice with lesson concepts. You may even prefer some of these activities to those used in the lesson. If so, substitute them or add them to the lesson.

If your school uses a grade-leveled approach to this curriculum, the lesson itself can be taught each year as the concepts bear repeating and students bring a new awareness level, new abilities to process, and new examples to each lesson. Use the following Supplementary Activities at these suggested grade levels:

1st   "Hatch a Friendly Dinosaur"
           (Supplementary Activity #1)
        "Friendship Words"
           (Supplementary Activity #2)
        "People Like You Better When You Are Nice To Them"
           (Supplementary Activity #3)

2nd   "A Perfect Friend for Me!"
           (Supplementary Activity #4)
        "A Class Friendship T-Shirt"
           (Supplementary Activity #5)

3rd   "My Idea of a Good Friend"
           (Supplementary Activity #6)
        "Our Group's Idea of What a Friend Should Be Like"
           (Supplementary Activity #7)

Lesson Presentation

Say or paraphrase: **Were going to be spending some time talking about friendship. For some people, making friends is easy. For others it's harder. Some kids have problems making friends because they do things that make other kids not like them. Whether you have a hard time with friendship or already have good friends, there are a lot of things you can learn in order to get along with people better. Were going to be studying exactly what people do in order to make friends and keep them. This doesn't mean that all of a sudden everyone will be your friend. No one has the time or energy to be a close friend to everyone, but each of you can learn to be close friends with one or a few other people.**

A STORY ABOUT TWO KIDS

Let me tell you a little story about two boys named Toni and Pat. It could be about two girls, too, and you can imagine it that way if you want to.

> Toni has tons of friends. Everyone likes to play with him at recess. Kids want to sit next to him at lunch. They like to be partners with him on class projects or field trips. They like to ask him over to their homes to play or have him sleep over. Toni has a knack for making friends. Its not that he's particularly good-looking or great at sports or schoolwork. He's just kind of an average kid BUT when it comes to friends, Toni does all the right things.
>
> Things are different for Pat. Kids stay away from him. No one plays with him at recess. No one wants to sit by him at lunch. No one asks him to be their partner on class projects or field trips. He doesn't get invited over to other kids' homes to play. Pat really isn't sure just why he has such bad luck making friends. All he knows is when he does try to do things to make friends, it doesn't work.

We'll talk another time about what Pat might be doing that keeps kids away. For now let's concentrate on why kids like Toni so well. The funny thing is that Toni doesn't really know what he does that causes kids to like him. He feels he was just being

himself. All he knows is that having friends isn't a problem for him.

STUDENTS BRAINSTORM FRIENDSHIP QUALITIES

Blank Transp.

Why do you think kids like Toni? What are some of the things he might be doing that make kids want to be around him? *Allow for student response. Students will probably say things like, "Because he's nice." Encourage them to be more specific or to give examples of friendly behaviors. You may want to write their responses on a blank transparency or the blackboard. As you do so, translate their examples into traits, saying something like,* **Acting like this could be described by the word _____.** *Try to use words like* shares, plays fair, good sport, honest, *etc. Sum up by saying,* **You're right, these are probably the type of things that Toni does.**

Just for fun, lets look at some more types of behaviors like these and see what most of you want a person to be like before you would choose them to be a friend.

STUDENTS VOTE ON FRIENDSHIP QUALITIES

Transp. #1
Transp. #2A

Show Transparency #1, "What We Want Most in a Friend." **Lets create sort of an imaginary perfect friend. I'm going to show you some words that describe what other kids have said they like in a friend.** *Put the four examples of the left arm cut out of Transparency #2A, "What We Want Most in a Friend—Words" (cut into pieces) on top of Transparency #1, right under the figure's left arm. Say:* **Here are four ways you might want a friend to be. You might want them to be <u>fair</u> and not cheat you; you might want them to be <u>talented</u> at something; it might be important to you that they are <u>smart</u>; or you might want a friend to be the <u>outdoorsy</u> type. Now I want each of you to decide which of these you would want most in a friend. All of these words are things that some kids want and you'll each have your opinion. There are not right or wrong answers. Think about it for a second. What do you want most in friends—that they play fair, or that they're talented, smart, or outdoorsy? Lets take a vote! Remember to only raise your hand one time.**

Transp. #2B

Say each of the four words, counting the number of hands up for each. Write that number next to the word on the arm. Some students may vote twice; if so, you'll have to do a recount. Write the winning quality on top of the blank arm on the figure on Transparency #1. Say something like, **Well, it looks as if in our class most kids think its important for a friend to be _____. Luckily, it looks as if you don't have to be _____ to have a friend in this class because it didn't get very many votes.** *Do the same for the other arms and legs and the T-shirt (Transparency #2B). When you have a completed figure, say:* **It looks like, if you want to have a friend in this class, its important to most kids that you be: _____.** *Read the words the students selected. You may want to write these words on the board or a chart under the heading "What We Want Most in a Friend."*

STUDENTS MAKE INDIVIDUAL "PERFECT FRIENDS"

Handout #1
Handout #2

Give students Handout #1, "What I Want Most in a Friend," and Handout #2, "Friendship Word List." **Some of you may disagree with some of the things that got the highest votes. You may feel that there's something else you insist on before you'll choose someone for a friend, and it wasn't on the list. I'm going to give you each a drawing that you can turn into a perfect friend for you. Write words that describe your perfect friend on the arms, legs, and T-shirt. You can use the "Friendship Word List" for ideas of other words if you want. There's even a bubble where you can have this friend saying something you'd like them to say. You can draw the hair and face, and then color and decorate this friend any way you want. When you're done, you can look at each other's and tell each other what is most important to you in a friend.**

When most students have completed their friend, ask for volunteers to share the words they selected for the right leg, left arm, etc. Note similarities between student responses by saying things like: **So, both Mary and Jim want a friend who is honest, a good sport, and fun.** *Note differences between student responses by saying things like:* **Sally and Dino have picked different words but they're both right. All of these words are important but each of you has your own ideas of what is most important to you in a friend. You may think it's more important to have a friend who is outdoorsy than under-**

standing. Someone else may feel just the opposite. This is good because it gives everyone a chance to find a friend. *You can have students use their completed "perfect friend" to decorate the cover of their Friendship Folder. They will use the Friendship Folder as a place to keep the handouts you'll be giving them during this friendship unit. Another option is to display the perfect friends and use Supplementary Activity #6, "My Idea of a Good Friend," as the cover for their folder.*

SURVEY OF STUDENTS WHO HAVE FRIENDSHIP BEHAVIORS

Now we've voted as a class on friendship behaviors that are important to us and you've created your own example of what you want in a friend. Next, I'd like you to do something else. I'd like you to think about kids in our class who are doing the kinds of behaviors that most kids seem to like.

Handout #3
Poster

Give students Handout #3, "Kids in Our Class Who Have Friendly Behaviors." You may also want to give students a class list to assist in spelling names. Introduce the handout by saying, **Think of someone in our class who is not selfish and is really good at sharing. Write their name in the first blank. Now, think of someone who is not always pouting or in a bad mood and is a lot of fun to be around.** *Go through the rest of the handout. Explain that you will share the results later (on the "Tally Sheet: Results of the Friendship Survey" Poster). Direct student's attention to the box at the bottom of the handout. Ask them to write down the friendship behavior they think they're best at and the behavior they need to work on the most. Explain that this will not be shared with the class.*

Suggest that students take a pen and write the behavior they think they need to improve in tiny letters in the middle of the inside of their hand. Explain that this will help them remember that they intend to try to work on this behavior. Tell them you will remind them at the beginning and end of each day to look for times they can use the friendship behavior they selected.

LESSON REVIEW

Review the lesson, asking students what they have learned. Use one or more of the Supplementary Activities as a homework assignment or to provide additional practice in the days ahead. See grade-level recommendations in the "To the Teacher" section.

TRANSPARENCY #1

What We Want Most in a Friend

TRANSPARENCY #2A

What We Want Most in a Friend—Words

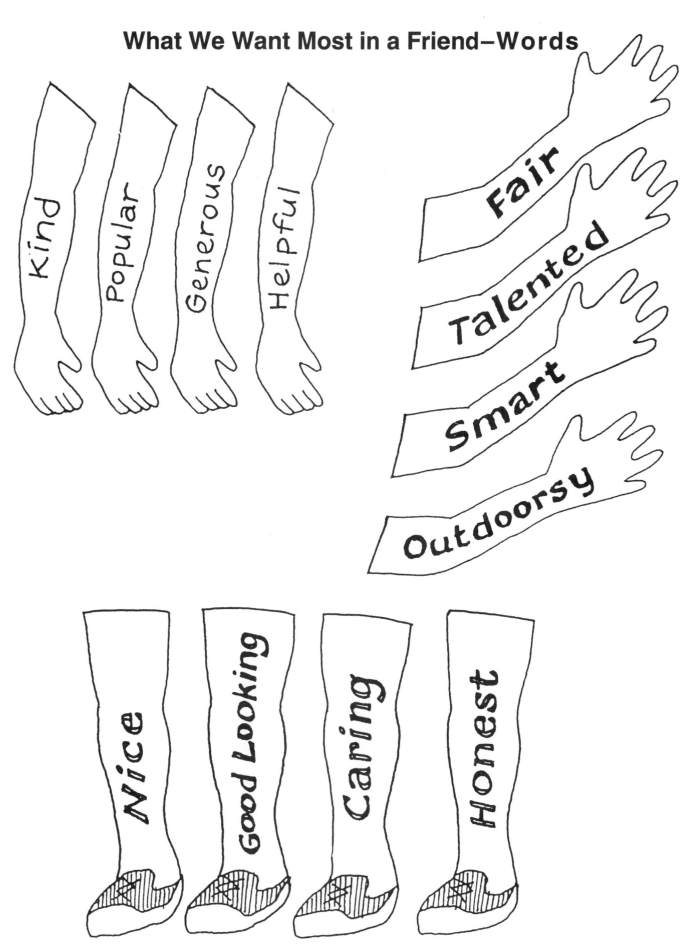

What We Want Most in a Friend—Words (continued)

What I Want Most in a Friend

Friendship Word List

caring	helpful
cheerful	honest
clever	imaginative
cooperative	kind
dependable	neat
easy-going	outdoorsy
fair	patient
forgiving	polite
fun	sharing
funny	talented
generous	thoughtful
good listener	understanding
good sport	unique

HANDOUT #3

Kids in Our Class Who Have Friendly Behaviors

1. Someone in this class who **shares** is _____ .

2. _____ is a lot of **fun**.

3. Someone in this class who is **helpful** to other is_____ .

4. _____ is an **honest** person.

5. A very **fair** person is _____ .

6. _____ is a **kind** person.

7. A **good sport** is_____ .

The friendship behavior I think **I'm best at is** _____ .

A friendship behavior I think **I need to work on** is _____ .

Teaching Friendship Skills: Primary Version

POSTER - TALLY SHEET

Results of the Friendship Survey

NAMES

Shares	
Fun	
Helpful	
Honest	
Fair	
Kind	
Good Sport	

Hatch a Friendly Dinosaur

NOTE: This activity creates a mobile.

Directions:

1. On each egg write two words that describe what is important to you in a friend. You can choose words from the list below or think up your own words.

2. Color the large dinosaur and the dinosaur eggs. (Very colorfully! Friendly dinosaurs come in all kinds of fun colors!)

3. Cut out the large dinosaur and dinosaur eggs along the dotted lines.

4. Fold the dinosaur and the eggs on the folding lines and glue them together.

5. Using a paper punch, punch holes at the dots (marked "⊗").

6. Hang the dinosaur eggs from the large dinosaur using loops of thread or string tied through the punched holes. Hang the eggs at different places on one piece of string.

7. Hang up your mobile, using thread or string tied to the top hole on the large dinosaur.

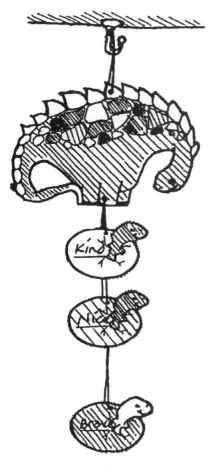

"I want my friends to be . . ."

brave
caring
fair
fun
good sports
helpful
honest
kind
nice
sharing

Hatch a Friendly Dinosaur

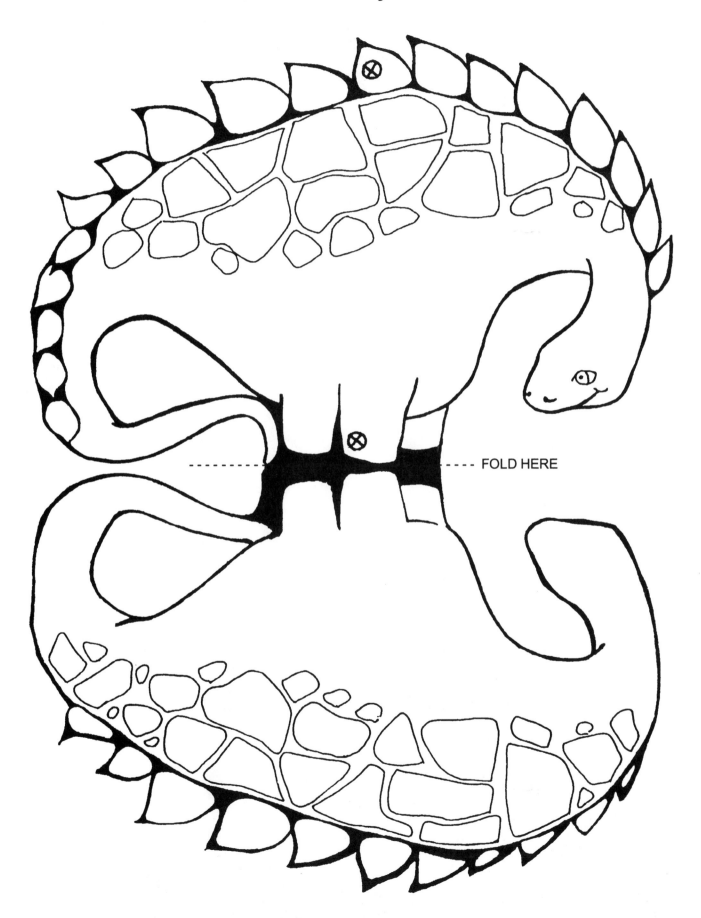

FOLD HERE

Hatch a Friendly Dinosaur–Eggs

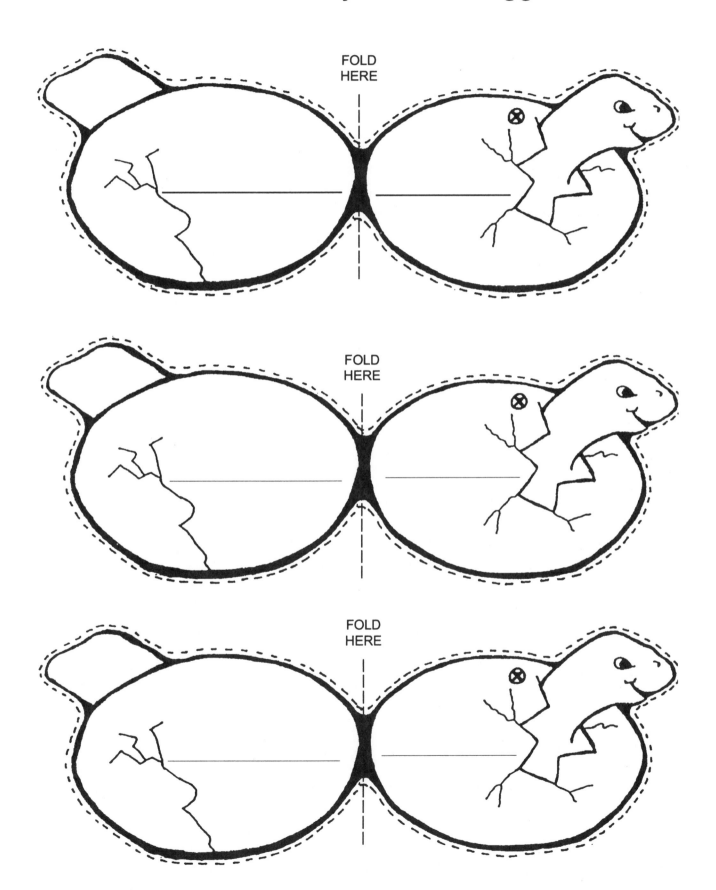

Friendship Words

Directions:

1. The words below describe ways people act when they want to have friends. **Trace over the letters of each word.** Then, ask yourself if you try to do what the word says. More kids will want to be your friend if you try to be **kind**, a **good sport**, **fair**, **understanding**, and if you **share**.

2. **Put a star** by the thing you do the best.

3. **Circle** the thing you want to try to do better.

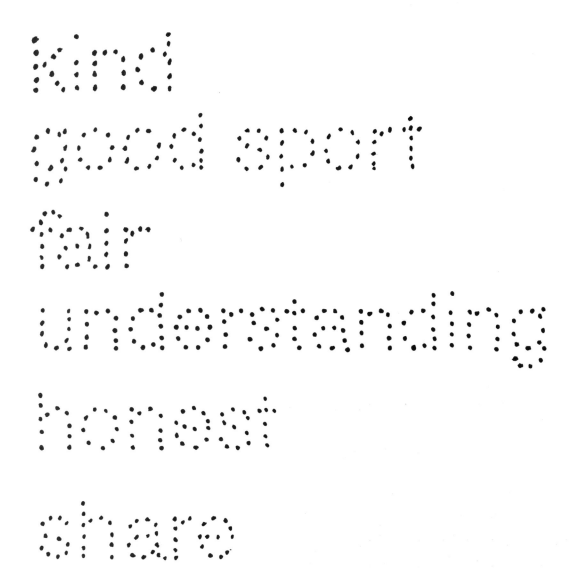

kind

good sport

fair

understanding

honest

share

People Like You Better When You Are Nice To Them

Directions:

Draw a picture that shows how you are a good friend.

"Would you like half of this?"

SUPPLEMENTARY ACTIVITY #4

A Perfect Friend for Me!

Objective Students identify the characteristics of a good friend by constructing a paper figure with the attributes they prefer.

Materials Supplementary Activity #4 Handout, "A Perfect Friend for Me!," for each student

Four very short-shank brads for each student

Scissors, crayons, and pencils

Procedure Tell students they will have an opportunity to construct their own "Perfect Friend." Distribute the handout and have students complete the facial features and hair; they are **not** to color the arms, legs, or clothing but should instead write behaviors or descriptors of their own choosing in the blanks provided. Emphasize that they are to think carefully and write qualities that describe their Perfect Friend. After completing the face and lettering, students should cut out the parts of their Friend. Have students carefully punch holes where the dots appear on the legs and arms. Students will lay the arms and legs on the trunk of their figure and put the brads through the holes. When the brads are spread, the arms and legs should move freely on the figure.

Figures can be displayed on a bulletin board or propped up on students' desks.

VARIATION

You may wish to dispense with the brads and have students glue the arms and legs onto their figure in a fixed position.

Teaching Friendship Skills: Primary Version
SUPPLEMENTARY ACTIVITY #4 HANDOUT

A Perfect Friend for Me!

Directions:

Fill in the blanks, color, then cut and pin together to make your perfect friend!

PIN
ARMS
& LEGS
TO BODY

Cares about:

Is good at:

Likes to:

Hates to:

Always:

Never:

Most of us would like to have a friend who likes the things we like, who cares about the things we think are important, and who is good at the things we enjoy.

SUPPLEMENTARY ACTIVITY #5

A Class Friendship T-Shirt

Objective

The student will demonstrate understanding of qualities of a good friend by contributing to the creation of a T-shirt or sweatshirt that characterizes a friendly person.

Materials

A large white T-shirt or sweatshirt

Various fabric paints, pens, and markers

Buttons, ties, trims, and ribbons (brought by students)

Needle, thread, safety pins

Sheet of cardboard

Handout #2, "Friendship Word List," from the lesson

Procedure

Tell students they will participate in designing a special Class Friendship T-Shirt and that they will be thinking and talking about some of the things that make a good friend. Lead students in deciding on words that characterize a good friend. They can use the "Friendship Word List" from the lesson for stimulus words. This may be done either as a class or in cooperative learning groups. In the latter case, each group would be asked to decide on their top two choices. Ask students to bring various trims from home to contribute to a cheerful and special-looking design for the T-shirt. Pull the T-shirt snugly over a sheet of cardboard and use various fabric paints and markers from your local craft supply store to write these friendship words on the T-shirt; trim the shirt whimsically with the things students bring from home. (You may wish to involve students in the design process to some degree.) When completed, the T-shirt should be a composite of the attributes the class values in a friend.

The T-shirt can be used in a variety of ways. Students may wish to nominate a classmate who has displayed good friendship behavior to wear the T-shirt for the day. Students who wish to do so may take turns wearing the T-shirt and focusing their efforts on good friendship behaviors. Students may draw names for the honor of wearing the T-shirt and being the "class friend." Another option is to allow a student who is having a bad day to decide to wear the T-shirt in order to focus on happier behaviors.

SUPPLEMENTARY ACTIVITY #6

My Idea of a Good Friend

Directions:

Think about those things that help you to choose a friend. **Write** one word in each balloon that tells what you want in a friend. You may use the Friendship Word List to help you. Next, **color or decorate** the balloons!

What I want in a good friend

Our Group's Idea of What a Friend Should Be Like

Directions:

Discuss with your group words that you think describe what a friend should be like. Have a group member write the words on the poster in the drawing.

Behaviors That Keep Kids From Having Friends

Objective   Students will learn behaviors that prevent the development of friendships by identifying behaviors they dislike in others.

Students will identify behaviors they have that interfere with friendships.

Materials   Blank transparencies and pen

Handout #1 - "Things Kids Do That Help or Hurt Friendships"

Transparency #1 - "How Much Does It Bug You?"

Transparency #2 - "You're Too Old to Still Be Hitting!"

Puppet Master #1 (Handouts #1-#4) - "Jesse Jackrabbit," made up in advance (or a puppet of your choice)

Puppet Master #2 (Handouts #1-#4) - "Marti Mouse," made up in advance (or a puppet of your choice)

Handout #2 - "Behaviors That Put a Wall between You and Other Kids"

Transparency #3A/Handout #3A - "Weeds"

Transparency #3B/Handout #3B - "Weeds"

Transparency #4 - "Unfriendly Behaviors"

Transparency #5A/Handout#4A - "Flowers"

Transparency #5B/Handout#4B - "Flowers"

Transparency #6 - "Friendly Behaviors"

Transparency #7 - "Raindrop Friendship Words" (also run off on blue paper and cut out for bulletin board display)

Handout #5 - "My Friendship Garden"

To the Teacher   In this lesson, students discuss what behaviors make them want to stay away from other kids. They vote on which behaviors "bug" them the most. They listen as two puppets have trouble with their friendship because of one of the puppet's alienating behaviors. (You can use the paper bag puppets included in this lesson or any other puppets you like.) After each puppet scenario, students brainstorm more appropriate interactions. You can use the puppets to demonstrate students' ideas or have them do so if you think they can do it effectively.

Students are given a handout where they are asked to take a look at themselves and rate how often they engage in anti-social behavior ("Behaviors That Put a Wall Between You and Other Kids," Handout #2). This is meant to be an awareness-raising exercise and students should not be asked to share their responses on this handout with their peers. This paper can be kept in their "Friendship Folder," which only you look at. They can remove this and any other handout that calls for this type of self-disclosure before sharing their Friendship Folder with family members.

If you're working with younger students and feel this lesson would be better for them if divided into two shorter sessions, a good stopping point would be after this activity (Handout #2).

In the "Friendship Garden" bulletin board activity suggested in this lesson, students are asked to notice and write down unfriendly things people do. These are written on "weeds" and put in the "class garden." This is another awareness-raising activity whereby students will become sensitized to behaviors that impede friendships. Students are also asked to notice friendly behaviors or prosocial comments. They write these down on "flowers" which can be used to replace the "weeds." The purpose of this is to promote the enactment of the positive behaviors taught in the last lesson.

Students are asked to analyze the types of behaviors or comments they make to others and make a private "Friendship Garden" (Handout #5). From this activity they are to generate a **goal** for behavior change for the days following the lesson. They are asked to use a "self-talk" statement and to write their goal on the palm of their hand as aids to remembering to work on their targeted behavior change. To facilitate transfer of training, ask students each morning and at the end of the school day to think of a specific time in the hours ahead when they can enact their goal.

Use one or more of the Supplementary Activities to reinforce the lesson concepts and provide practice. You may also substitute these if you find you prefer some of the Supplementary Activities to the activities suggested in the lesson.

If you are using this curriculum in a grade-leveled format, the following are the suggested grade-level activities:

1st   "Words That Make or Break Friendships"
          (Supplementary Activity #1)
       "Friendly or Unfriendly?"
          (Supplementary Activity #2)

2nd "Grade Yourself As A Friend"
     (Supplementary Activity #3)
    "Find the Friendly Bunnies"
     (Supplementary Activity #4)

3rd "Being FRIENDS Means . . ."
     (Supplementary Activity #5)
    "Would You Pick These Kids For A Friend?"
     (Supplementary Activity #6)
    "Friendship Discussion Cards"
     (Supplementary Activity #7)

Lesson Presentation

REVIEW OF LESSON 1

`Blank Transp.`

Say or paraphrase: **Remember last week when we talked about the kid, Toni, who had such a knack for making friends? We made some guesses about why other kids liked him so much. Then we voted on the things we think are most important in a friend. Who can remember some of the things we decided were really important in a friend?** *Allow for student response, prompting if necessary. Write responses on a blank transparency.*

`Handout #1`
`Blank Transp.`

Distribute Handout #1, "Things Kids Do That Help or Hurt Friendships." **You also each decided what things were most important to you in choosing someone to be your friend. Fold your paper in half so only the top half shows. Stop a minute and think about things kids do that make you want to be their friend. Write these things on the board behind the boy on your paper.** *Ask students to share some of the friendship qualities they have written. Write these on a blank transparency or on the chalkboard. Ask students not to turn their papers to the bottom half until instructed to do so.*

Today we're going to talk about the other kid, Pat, who had so much trouble making friends. You can imagine Pat as either a boy or a girl. Remember, Pat was the kid that no one wanted to play with at recess or sit next to at lunch. No one wanted to be partners with Pat on school projects or on field trips. Kids didn't invite Pat over to their houses to play. Pat wasn't really sure why it was so hard to make friends. It just seemed like anything Pat did to try to make friends didn't work.

STUDENTS BRAINSTORM ALIENATING BEHAVIORS

Blank Transp.

Let's make some guesses about what Pat might be doing wrong. What are some of the things Pat might be doing that drive other kids away? *Allow for student response. List their responses on a blank transparency.*

Yep! I think you've nailed down some of the behaviors that would make kids not want to be around Pat. Turn your paper to the bottom half now and think for a minute about things kids do that make you not want to be their friend. Write these things down on the board behind the boy on your paper. *Ask students to share some of the things they've written. Have students slip these papers into their Friendship Folders.*

STUDENTS VOTE ON BEHAVIORS THAT INTERFERE WITH FRIENDSHIP

Transp. #1

You've come up with a lot of behaviors kids do that keep them from having friends. *Put Transparency #1, "How Much Does It Bug You?," on the overhead.* **Just for fun, let's take a vote on some of the things other kids do that "bug" you most. I'll read through the list and you be thinking of the five things that "bug" you the most. Then I'll read the list again, and you can vote on your top five.**

Read the items and tally votes next to each item on the transparency. After the vote, comment on behaviors that are particularly unpopular by saying things like, "Well, it looks like if you want to have a friend in this class, you'd better not be a tattle-tale," or "You can see from the vote that in this class kids really don't like someone who's bossy," or "If you haven't learned to keep your hands to yourself by now, this vote ought to convince you that kids hate it when someone pokes or hits them," or "As you can see, it really bugs kids to be called names." Say: **My guess is these are probably the kinds of things Pat did that drove other kids away.**

ROLE-PLAYING NEGATIVE BEHAVIORS USING PUPPETS

Puppets

I've brought a couple of friends along to help us today. *Show puppets.* **This is Jesse Jackrabbit and this is Marti Mouse. You can imagine that they are boy or girl animals. Jesse and Marti are classmates in a room similar to this one, only Jesse and Marti are having some trouble learning how to be friends. Watch what happens in this scene:**

Use the following puppet-play scenarios to dramatize the effects of negative behaviors on friendships. (Although most children are aware that hitting and pushing are unacceptable, many don't realize how much other behaviors such as tattling, wanting to be the center of attention, criticizing, and bossiness also alienate their peers.)

SCENARIO I—TATTLING

It's math time in Jesse Jackrabbit and Marti Mouse's classroom. Jesse goes to the pencil sharpener. On the way back to her seat, Jesse passes Marti working at his desk. Without stopping, Jesse reaches over and, just as a joke, makes a mark at the top of Marti's math paper. Jesse snickers and sits down in her seat in front of Marti.

Marti: **You rat! You made a mark on my paper! I'm gonna tell!**

Jesse: **Don't make such a big deal of it! It's just a little mark. You can erase it.**

Marti: **I don't want to erase it. I'm going to tell the teacher!**

Jesse: **Good grief, Marti. Cool your jets!**

Marti: **Mr. Otto! Mr. Otto! Jesse ruined my paper. She marked all over it! LOOK!**

Would you want to be friends with Marti Mouse? Why or why not? Even though it wasn't very nice of Jesse to have made a mark on Marti's paper, what could Marti have done differently?

Lead students to realize that Marti could have expressed appropriate anger to Jesse. Marti could have told Jesse he didn't like what Jesse did and not to do it again. It wasn't necessary for Marti to tattle. Dramatize the scene again showing Marti expressing anger directly to Jesse in an assertive yet nonattacking way.

Summarize by saying, **Kids who tattle about every little thing make other kids mad. No one wants to be around a tattle-tale.**

Watch this next scene and see if you can spot the problem.

SCENARIO II—WANTING TO BE THE CENTER OF ATTENTION

Jesse Jackrabbit has just returned from a trip with her parents. Several classmates are gathered around her before school, asking about the trip. Marti Mouse is in the group.

Jesse:	**There were some really high mountains there. We had to wear boots all the time because of the snow. One day . . .**
Marti:	**That's nothing! I was at my grandma's once and it snowed 18 inches in one night. You should have seen the snow! We could hardly get out the door.**
Jesse:	**Well, anyway, one day my sister and I were playing outside. She stepped into a deep drift and sank to her knees. When my dad lifted her out, both her boots stuck in the snow and came off! My dad had to . . .**
Marti:	**That's nothing! One time my dad was icefishing and he sank to his waist in freezing water. He almost froze before he got out!**
Jesse:	**Anyway, I got my first time ever to ride a bobsled. Boy, was that fun! It was a flat wooden sled that curled up in front and . . .**

(continued)

Marti:	**I've got a sled! When it snows I take it down the hill in front of my house; it goes about 100 miles an hour!**
Jesse:	*(heavy sigh)* **My dad and us three kids piled on that sled. On the way down the hill, we hit a bump and all four of us fell out in a pile with my dad on the bottom. We thought it was fun, but my dad . . .**
Marti:	**Let me tell you about the time I crashed MY sled! There was this ditch by the side of the road, and . . .**
Jesse:	**Hey, I'll talk to the rest of you guys about my trip later . . . .** *(Jesse leaves.)*

What happened here? What was Marti doing that bugged Jesse? Would that behavior make kids want to be friends with him? Why do you think Marti kept interrupting and trying to be the center of attention? *Help students realize that Marti probably wanted to belong.* **What could Marti have done instead that would have made Jesse and the others feel O.K. about Marti being in the group?**

Allow for student response. If necessary, model for students appropriate ways of inserting comments in a conversation and waiting for a turn to speak. Dramatize the scene again with Marti being a better listener and waiting for his turn to talk. Then summarize by saying, **Kids would like Marti more if Marti wasn't always trying to be the center of attention.**

Watch this next scene and see another thing kids do that make other kids not like them.

SCENARIO III—BOSSINESS

Jesse and Marti were chosen by the teacher to make a bulletin board display. They're supposed to work together and share ideas.

(continued)

> *Marti:* **I've got this all figured out. I want the background to be blue and the letters to be purple.**
>
> *Jesse:* **But, Marti. It's hard to see purple on blue from a distance.**
>
> *Marti:* **Here, take this purple paper and cut out the letters for me.**
>
> *Jesse:* **How about using red? It would look nice on blue.**
>
> *Marti:* **Red, YUK! Use the purple. Start cutting the letters and be careful on the corners so you don't wreck them!**
>
> *Jesse:* **I think when we put the letters up they should go under each picture.**
>
> *Marti:* **No. We'll do it my way. I always put the letters over the pictures!**
>
> *Jesse:* **Humph . . . .**

What do you suppose Jesse was thinking when she said, "Humph?" Would you want to work with Marti? Do you think Jesse would want Marti for a friend? Why? If you were Marti and thought you had some good ideas about the bulletin board but didn't want to lose Jesse as a friend, what are some things you could have said as you went about this project? How could you have suggested your ideas without being bossy? *Use the puppets to dramatize student responses or allow students with valuable suggestions to dramatize them if you feel it would be effective modeling for the rest of the class. Ask the class which responses they like the best and would make Marti a fun partner to work with. Summarize by saying:* **Nobody wants a bossy kid for a friend. You can express your opinions, listen to other people's opinions, and work out ways of doing things so that you both get part of what you want.**

You've done a good job figuring out things kids say that wreck friendships and suggesting things that kids could say that would make others want to be their friend.

STUDENTS THINK ABOUT HOW OFTEN THEY DO THINGS THAT ALIENATE THEIR PEERS

Handout #2

Let's take a few minutes to think about our own behavior and ask ourselves if we do things that make it hard for kids to be our friends. You could say that the kind of behaviors we've been talking about today keep other kids away or put a wall between kids. *Give students Handout #2, "Behaviors That Put a Wall Between You and Other Kids." Read through the instructions with students. Model doing this yourself by saying something like:* **Well, in the "Hitting" brick, I can give myself an "n." I've gotten over hitting—I never do it anymore. In the "Bossing" brick, though, I would give myself an "s" because I'm still bossy at home sometimes.** *Point out that they will not be sharing this paper with the other students. It will go in their Friendship Folders and they will be coloring their bricks red so their marks won't show. Explain that the only purpose for doing this activity is to help students stop and think about how often they do unfriendly things and which behavior they need to change so they will have more friends.*

NOTE: *If you want to break this lesson into two sessions, this would be a good ending point for the first session.*

BULLETIN BOARD ACTIVITY FOCUSING ON FRIENDLY AND UNFRIENDLY BEHAVIORS IN THE CLASSROOM AND ON THE PLAYGROUND

Wouldn't it be wonderful to have a classroom where no one said anything unfriendly? If we could weed out all the unfriendly things kids say, our room would be a happy place for everyone!

Transp. #3A
Transp. #3B

Let's make a bulletin board and pretend it's a garden. Let's pretend that this garden hasn't been cared for and has some ugly, prickly weeds in it. *Show Transparency #3A and #3B, "Weeds," on the overhead.*

I'm going to put out some copies of weeds like these, and when you see any unfriendly behaviors in our classroom like the ones we've been talking about, I want you to write down what you saw on one of these weeds. Don't use any names; just write down

what happened that wasn't friendly. In your free time, you can color the weed and pin it up. Let's each do one weed now just for practice.

Handout #3A
Handout #3B

Give students a copy of Handout #3A, "Weeds" (same as transparency). Make other copies of Handouts #3A and #3B available for students to use in the days ahead. **On one of the weeds write down something unfriendly you've seen or heard in the past.**

Transp. #4

Show Transparency #4, "Unfriendly Behaviors." **You might have heard someone say something <u>bossy</u>, like, "Do it my way or I won't play!" You might have heard someone say, "I'm going to tell the teacher!" so you might write "<u>tattling</u>" on your weed. You might write "<u>teasing</u>" because you've heard someone say, "You've got a girlfriend!"**

You might have seen someone <u>break a promise</u>. Maybe you'll write about a <u>selfish</u> thing you saw or heard, like, "I want to use the best one first!" You might write down "<u>wanting to be the center of attention</u>" because you heard someone say, "That's nothing—listen to what I did!" You might write "<u>lying</u>" on your weed because you remember a time when you saw a kid cut in line and they lied, saying, "I didn't cut into line—my friend saved this place for me." You might also want to write one of the "Baby Behaviors" if you've seen these happen in our class or on the playground.

These are just a few examples. I'm sure you can think of other weed-like things that have hurt kids' feelings and have kept kids from being good friends. Don't use any names, just write what you saw or heard on one weed now.

In the days ahead, be watching for any unfriendly behaviors in our classroom, on the playground, or in the lunchroom. If you see one, write it on a weed and we'll put it in our garden. *After students have completed, colored, and cut out one of the three weeds on Handout #3A, pin or tape the weeds on the "Friendship Garden" bulletin board. Have them put the rest of the "Weeds" handout in their Friendship Folder for them to use the next time they observe an unfriendly behavior.*

Transp. #5A
Handout #4A
Transp. #5B
Handout #4A

Show students Transparencies #5A and #5B, "Flowers." Give students copies of Handouts #4A and #4B. Have other copies of these handouts available for use in the days ahead. Say: **We also have flowers for our garden. Guess what we're going to write on those?** *Allow for student response.* **Right! Friendly behaviors! Whenever you see someone in our class doing something kind or something that makes someone else feel good, you can get one of these flowers and write on it what they did or said. When I give you free time, you can color the flower and put it up in our garden.**

Transp. #6

Let's do one now. Think of a friendly behavior you've seen or heard someone do. *Show Transparency #6, "Friendly Behaviors." Read through this transparency as you did on the previous one, "Unfriendly Behaviors," pointing out that students have probably seen at least one example of either sharing, helping, being fair, caring, complimenting, or apologizing which they could write down on a flower. Remind students not to use any names. (You might want to allow students to put names of those they observed doing a friendly behavior on the flowers.)*

Place the completed flowers in the Friendship Garden along with the weeds. Ask students to be on the watch for friendly behaviors in the days ahead. Just like they will do for the weeds and unfriendly behaviors— except they won't use any names on the weeds. When they see a friendly behavior they can get a flower, write down what they saw or heard, and put it up in the garden. Establish your own rules regarding when you want students to write out their weeds and flowers and place them in the Friendship Garden. Point out that it will be interesting to see if the garden accumulates more flowers or more weeds in the days ahead.

Transp. #7

Show Transparency #7, "Raindrop Friendship Words." Say: **We'll water the flowers in our garden with these raindrops. They have some of the friendship words on them that we learned last week, remember? These words describe things that help friendships grow.** *(You could put the raindrops on the "Friendship Bulletin Board.")*

Handout #5

Give students Handout #5, "My Friendship Garden." **Besides this classroom Friendship Garden we'll be making, I'd like you each to make your own private garden. I'd like you to write on each of these flowers something you have said or done that was friendly, or something you could say or do that would make someone feel good and want to be your friend. Then, on each** weed, write down something you have said or done that would keep someone from being your friend.

Next, pick the weed that you would most like to get rid of. Decide what you're going to do to get that weed out of your garden. Write what you'll do really small inside the palm of your hand and on the space for it below the "Weed Patch" on your paper. Some of you will write "I won't tease." Others will write "I won't be bossy," or "I won't hit." Some of you might write "I won't give put-downs." Whatever you put on your hand is the behavior you should be working on between now and our next friendship lesson.

What is something you could say to yourself that would help you remember to work on this behavior? *Guide students in generating helpful self-talk statements. Suggest:* **Some things you might say are:**

- **Kids will like me better if I . . . .**
- **People don't like it when I . . . .**
- **I don't like it when people do this to me so I shouldn't do it to others.**
- **I'll have more friends if I . . . .** *Etc.*

When students are done with their Friendship Garden handouts they can put them in their Friendship Folders.

LESSON REVIEW

Review the lesson, asking students what they have learned. In addition, you might want to use the following sentence stems:

- *I was surprised . . . .*
- *I liked . . . .*
- *I didn't like . . . .*

Use one or more of the Supplementary Activities as a homework assignment or to provide additional practice in the days ahead. See grade-level recommendations in the "To the Teacher" section at the beginning of this lesson.

Things Kids Do That Help or Hurt Friendships

Things kids do that make me WANT to be their friend.

Things kids do that make me NOT want to be their friend.

How Much Does It BUG You?

When someone . . .

1. Is always "tattling"?
2. Laughs when you make a mistake?
3. Won't make up after fights?

Directions:
Circle the 5 things that bug you the most. Put a star by the 2 very worst ones.

4. Is a copycat?
5. Bosses you around?
6. Won't share his or her things with you?

7. Tells your secrets?
8. Always pokes or hits you?
9. Has to always have his or her way?

10. Calls you names?
11. Acts silly all the time?
12. Has to be the center of attention?
13. Doesn't play fair?

14. Talks too much?
15. Tells lies?

You're Too Old to Still Be Hitting!

**Hitting
Kicking
Pushing
Shoving
Poking
and
Pinching
are for
BABIES.**

☞ **Kids your age are too old to be doing these things.**

– When you were very little you didn't know any better than to hit, kick, push, shove, poke, or pinch.

– By the time kids get out of preschool, they should let people know they're mad by telling them.

☞ **Kids your age can show you're mad, strong, and tough by using WORDS!**

"Cut it out!"

You can say things like:

- "Stop it!"
- "Leave me alone!"
- "Don't do that!"
- "That makes me mad!"
- "Stop bugging me!"
- "Knock it off!"

PUPPET MASTER #1 HANDOUT #1

Jesse Jackrabbit

Directions:

1. Glue the head onto a piece of stiff paper (or copy onto stiff paper), so the ears won't be too floppy.

2. Color the head, body front (with mouth), and body back.

3. Cut out the pieces.

4. Glue a cotton ball on the tail area.

5. Glue the front and back of the body to the front and back of the paper bag (use a standard Size #6 lunch sack, 5-3/8" x .10-3/4").

6. Glue the head onto the bottom of the paper bag, as shown in A.

7. Use your hand to make the puppet talk, as shown in B.

Jesse Jackrabbit: Head

PUPPET MASTER #1 HANDOUT #3

Jesse Jackrabbit: Body Front

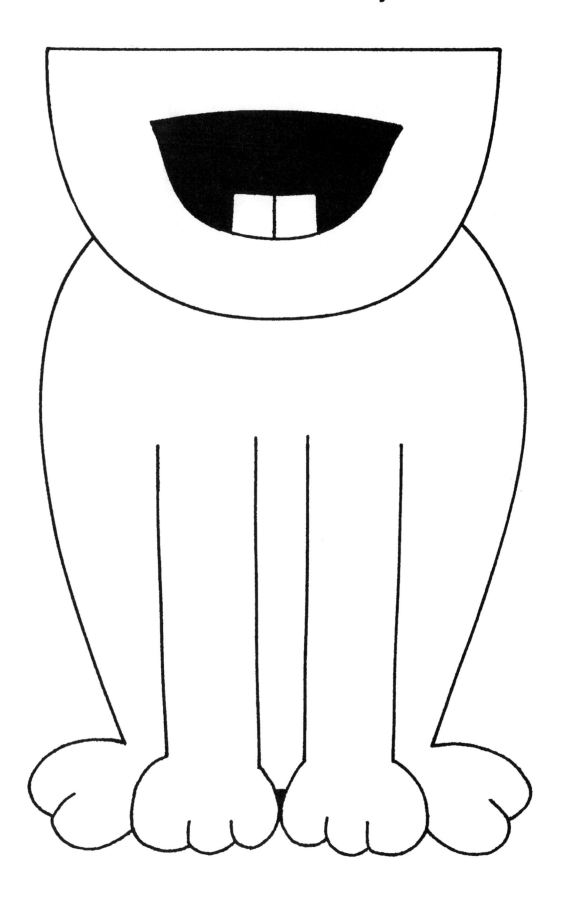

Jesse Jackrabbit: Body Back

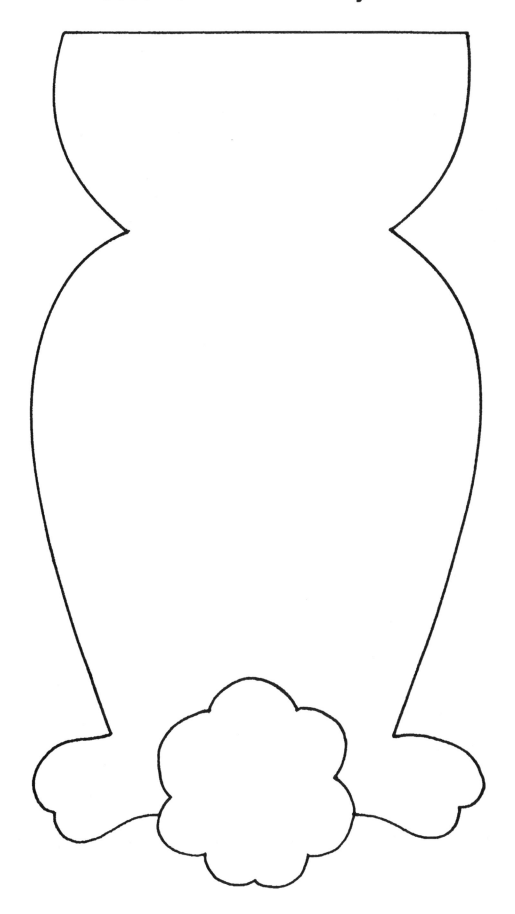

Marti Mouse

Directions:

1. Glue the head onto a piece of stiff paper (or copy onto stiff paper), so the ears won't be too floppy.

2. Color the head, body front (with mouth), and body back.

3. Cut out the pieces.

4. Punch out a hole for the tail (marked "⊗") and tie on a rubber band to make Marti's tail.

5. Glue the front and back of the body to the front and back of the paper bag (use a standard Size #6 lunch sack, 5-3/8" x .10-3/4").

6. Glue the head onto the bottom of the paper bag, as shown in A.

7. Use your hand to make the puppet talk, as shown in B.

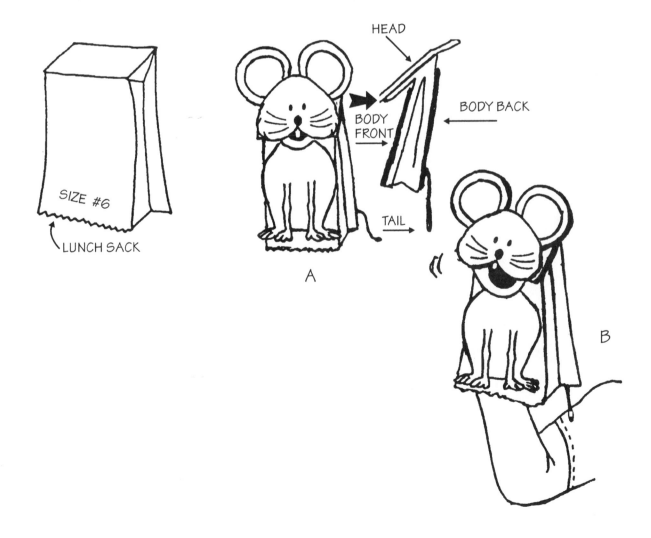

PUPPET MASTER #2 HANDOUT #2

Marti Mouse: Head

Marti Mouse: Body Front

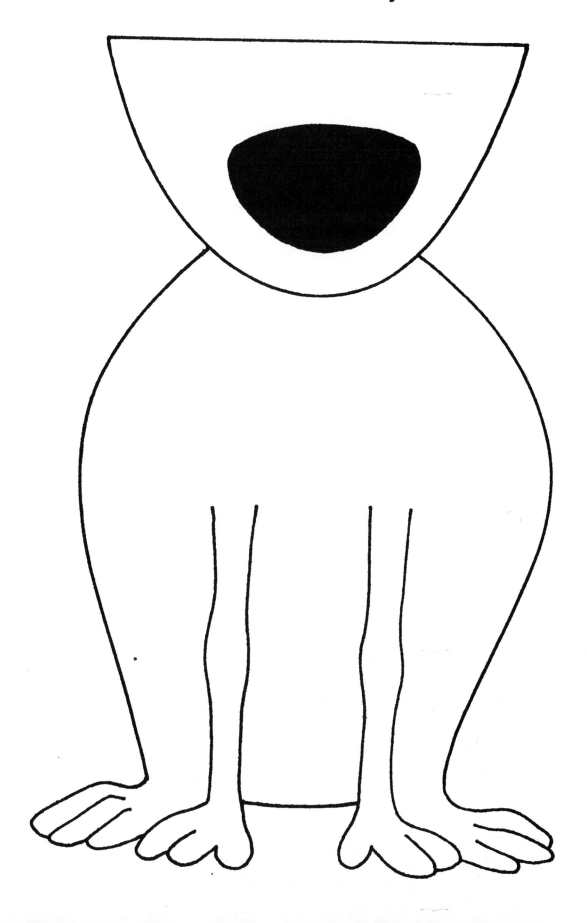

Teaching Friendship Skills: Primary Version

PUPPET MASTER #2 HANDOUT #4

Marti Mouse: Body Back

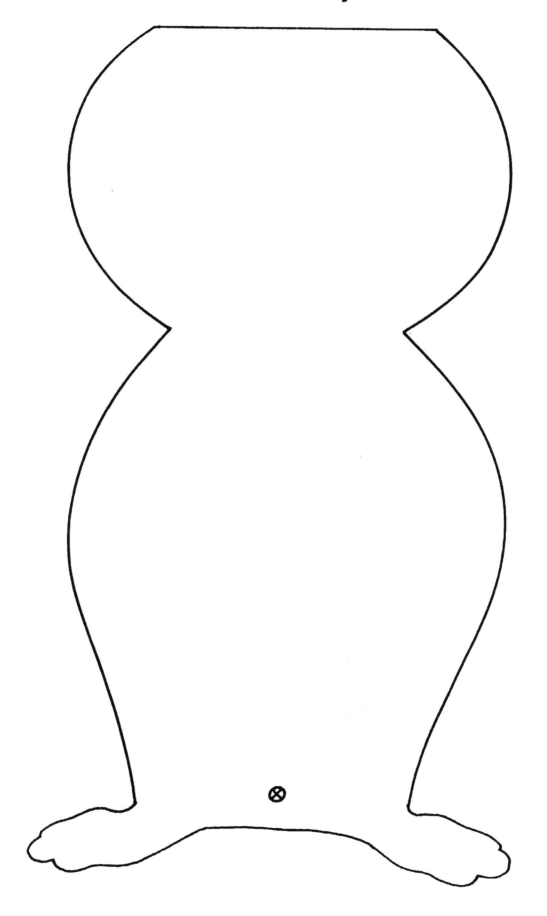

HANDOUT #2

Behaviors That Put a Wall Between You and Other Kids

The behaviors listed below are ones kids say they don't like. Most kids don't want to be around kids who do these things. You could say that these behaviors build a wall between kids.

Directions:

Ask yourself how often you do the things listed on the bricks of the wall.

— If you **never** do the behavior, circle the "n."

— If you **sometimes** do the behavior, circle the "s."

— If you **often** do the behavior, circle the "o."

Teaching Friendship Skills: Primary Version

TRANSPARENCY #3A/HANDOUT #3A

Weeds

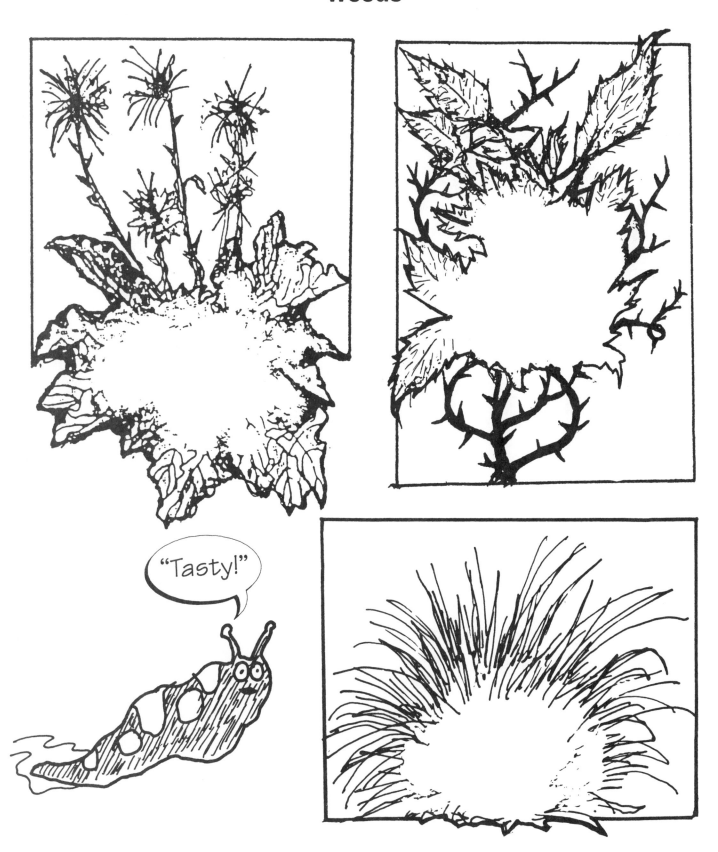

Weeds (continued)

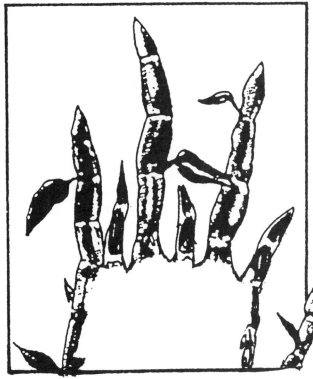

Unfriendly Behaviors

Bossiness
"Do it my way or I won't play!"

Tattling
"I'm going to tell the teacher!"

Teasing
"You've got a girlfriend!"

Breaking Promises
"I don't care if I said I would—I'm not going to!"

Selfishness
"I want to use the best one first!"

Wanting to Be the Center of Attention
"That's nothing—listen to what I did!"

Lying
"I didn't cut into line—my friend saved this place for me."

The "Baby Behaviors"

Hitting	Shoving
Kicking	Poking
Pushing	Pinching

Flowers

Flowers (continued)

Friendly Behaviors

Sharing
"Here, you use the best one."
"Want half of my snack?"

Helping
"Do you want some help?"
"I'll show you how, if you like."

Being Fair
"It's your turn to go first."
"Oops! I missed. You win."

Caring
"Don't feel bad; everybody makes mistakes."
"Keep trying; you'll probably do better next time."

Complimenting
"You did a good job on that."
"You're fun to play with."

Apologizing
"I'm sorry."
"I didn't mean to hurt you."

Raindrop Friendship Words

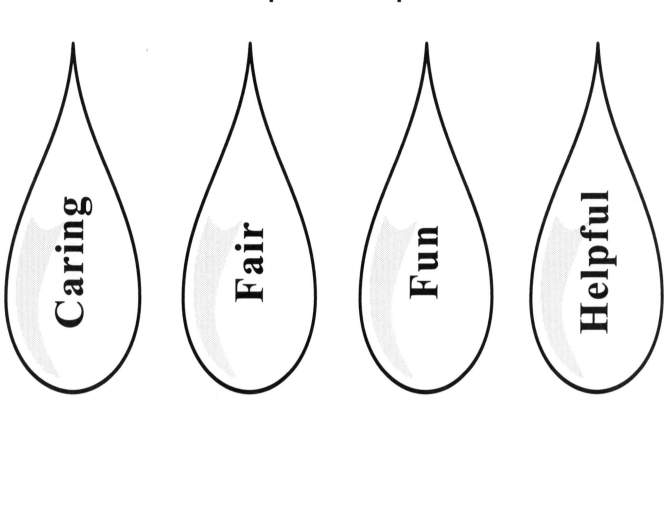

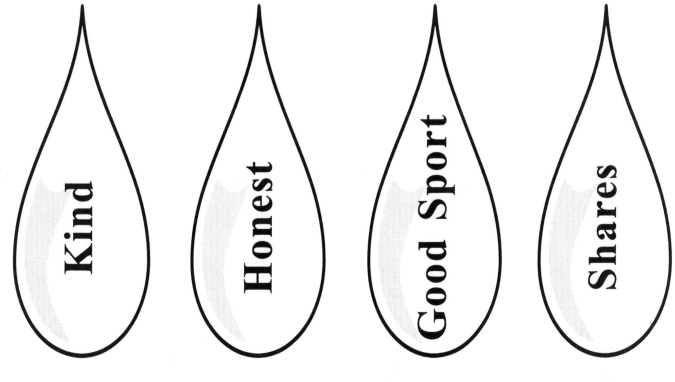

My Friendship Garden

"I like to chew up friendships."

"Tasty!"

The Weed Patch:
Things I say sometimes that **don't help** me make friends.

The Flower Bed:
Things I say that **help** me make friends.

The behavior I'll be working on this week is:

Words That Make or Break Friendships

Directions:

Draw a 🙂 in the shapes with words that **help** friendships.

Draw a ☹ in the shapes with words that **don't** help friendships.

Circle the two friendship words you think are the most important.

Color the shapes.

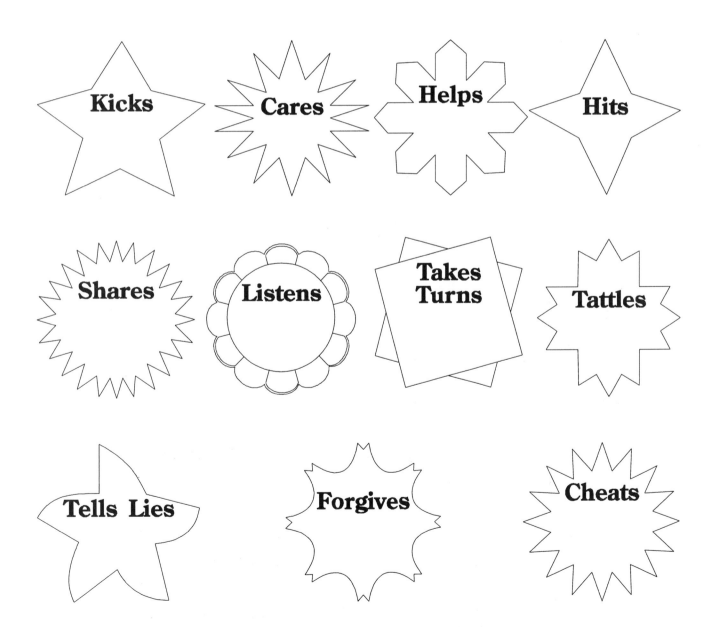

Friendly or Unfriendly?

Objective   Students will differentiate between friendly and unfriendly behaviors by deciding whether various behaviors and phrases promote or impede friendships.

Materials   Two large sheets of paper, labeled "Friendly" and "Unfriendly"

Glue stick

Supplementary Activity #2 Handouts #1A and #1B, "Friendly or Unfriendly?" Cards, cut apart

Procedure   Cut the sentence cards apart. Add sentences of your own to the blank cards, if you like. Place the two large "Friendly" and "Unfriendly" sheets at the front of the room. Tell the students you need their help making a class list of the kinds of things kids say when they're being friendly and the things they say when they're being unfriendly.

Place the sentence cards in a stack on a table and demonstrate by drawing a card, reading it aloud, telling the class whether it's a friendly or unfriendly statement (and perhaps why you think so). Then, put glue on the back of the card, and stick it to the appropriate sheet. Have students come up, draw a card, and follow your modeling. You can read the card for them. When the charts are completed, encourage children to use the kinds of sentences that are on the "Friendly" chart when they are with others.

VARIATION 1

You may wish to extend this activity over several days by selecting only five students at a sitting and allowing for class discussion of each strip.

VARIATION 2

After the activity is completed, you may wish to provide a stack of blank cards for students to write on in the ensuing days as they overhear friendly and unfriendly comments. These cards can be added to the sheets as either a structured or unstructured activity.

Friendly or Unfriendly? Cards

You did a good job!	I want the biggest piece!
Let's look at this book together.	Why don't you go play somewhere else?
Could I have it back, please?	Your picture looks dumb.
If you don't let me go first, I won't play.	Let's trade baseball cards.
We don't want you to play with us.	That's nothing—listen to what I did!
Let's pretend we're horses.	You push me on the swing and then I'll push you.
Let's use your Legos and my Legos together, and we'll make a farm.	Do you want some help?
I'm better at that than you are.	You're fun to play with!
You missed, but you tried hard.	Do you want to share my colors?

(Legos™)

SUPPLEMENTARY ACTIVITY #2 HANDOUT #1B

Friendly or Unfriendly? Cards (continued)

You can't draw! Let me do it.	You say your idea first, then I'll say mine.
Sure, you can use it.	I'd like my jump rope back. Here's your ball.
Don't touch those. They're mine.	You don't get any.
You can ride on it for awhile.	That's nothing special—listen to what happened to me!
I'm going to tell the teacher on you!	I'm sorry.
Your shirt looks weird.	I'll give you some of my candy if you'll give me some of your gum.

SUPPLEMENTARY ACTIVITY #3

Grade Yourself As A Friend

Directions: Below are some of the behaviors of a friend. Grade yourself in each area.	**A** **Excellent**	**B** **Very Good**	**C** **Average**	**D** **Needs Improve-ment**
1. I share				
2. I play fair				
3. I help others				
4. I don't hit or push				
5. I don't put people down				
6. I'm not bossy				
7. I don't tattle				

Find the Friendly Bunnies

Directions:

1. **Draw** a line between the words that are opposites.

2. **Color** in the bunnies that have words on them that would help them make friends.

3. **Put an "X" across** the bunnies that would not make good friends.

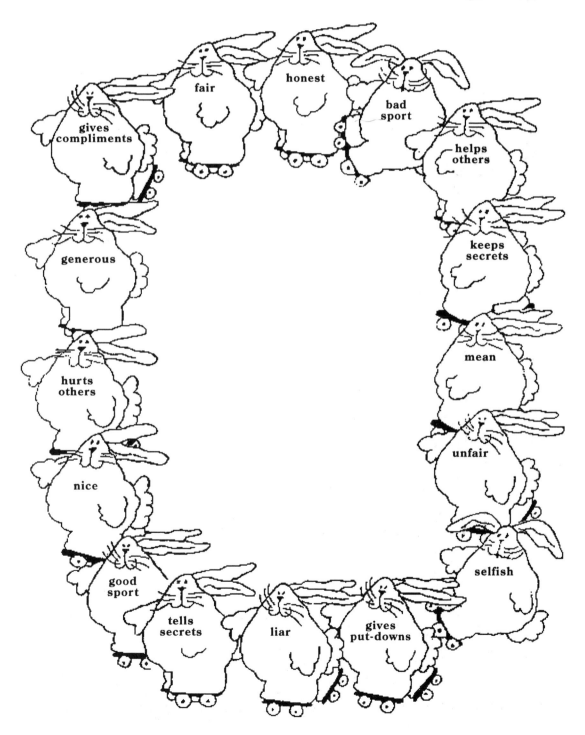

SUPPLEMENTARY ACTIVITY #4 ANSWER SHEET

Find the Friendly Bunnies–Answer Sheet

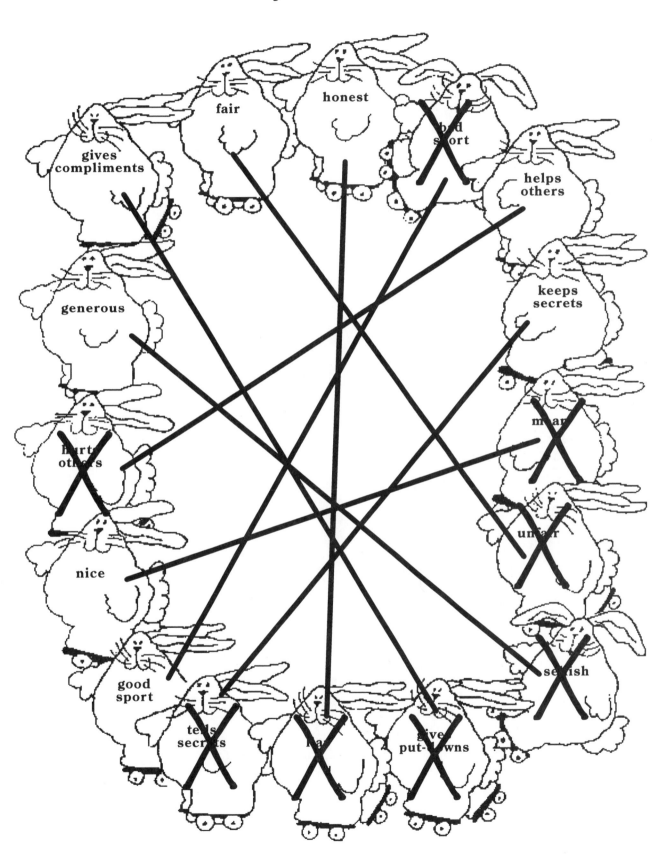

SUPPLEMENTARY ACTIVITY #5

Being FRIENDS Means . . .

Directions:

1. **Circle** the statements you agree with.

2. **Put an "X" through** the statements you don't agree with.

3. **Add your own ideas** about what being friends means in the boxes.

Being Friends Means . . .

Staying mad after a fight.

Listening when your friend has a problem.

Accepting someone the way they are and not trying to change them.

Not showing it when you're sad.

Not lying to each other.

Telling your friends when they bug you.

Telling secrets.

Using your friend's stuff whenever you want to.

Learning new things from each other.

Standing up for each other.

Having fun together.

Always doing what your friends want you to do.

Never getting mad at each other.

Noticing the good things your friends do and telling them.

1.

2.

3.

SUPPLEMENTARY ACTIVITY #6

Would You Pick These Kids For A Friend?

- **Rex** gets upset over every little thing. No matter what happens, he always seems to be complaining. He's in a grouchy mood most of the time.

    – Would you choose Rex to be your friend? _____

    – Why or why not? _____

    – What suggestions would you give to Rex so that people would like him better? _____

- **Lila** always thinks she is right. Even when she is wrong, she won't admit it. She always wants her own way and won't play unless she gets it.

    – Would you choose Lila to be your friend? _____

    – Why or why not? _____
    _____

    – What suggestions would you give to Lila so that people would like her better?_____
    _____

- **Vance** can't keep his hands to himself. He's always shoving, poking, pushing, or hitting someone. He never thinks how it would feel to have kids do this to him.

    – Would you choose Vance to be your friend? _____

    – Why or why not? _____

    – What suggestions would you give to Vance so that people would like him better? _____
    _____

- **Stella** thinks she is the best, and she always likes to be the center of attention. Whenever her friends tell her something good about themselves, Stella says "That's nothing—you should see what **I** did!"

    – Would you choose Stella to be your friend? _____
    – Why or why not? _____
    _____

    – What suggestions would you give to Stella so that people would like her better? _____

Friendship Discussion Cards

Objective   Students will brainstorm and compare ideas with their peers on various friendship topics.

Materials   Supplementary Activity #7 Handouts #1A and #1B - "Friendship Discussion Cards"

Animals from cards, duplicated and enlarged

Procedure   There are a variety of ways these cards can be used to spark discussion in your classroom:

- Duplicate and cut apart cards. Walk around the classroom, stopping here and there to have a student draw a card, read it aloud, and respond. (You may wish to allow students to draw a second card if they find their first draw too difficult.) If another student has a different response to the card drawn, you may call on him or her also.
- Duplicate the card sheets. Enlarge the animals in the corner of each of the eight cards and cut these out into squares of paper. Divide the class into cooperative learning groups, giving each group the two sheets of discussion cards. Allow each group to draw one of the squares with the animals; the animal drawn determines which discussion card will be theirs to discuss. Cooperative learning groups will then work together on that topic, brainstorming ideas and generating examples. The group "Recorder" will write their best answers on the Discussion Card and also will report their results to the rest of the class at the appropriate time. (Groups who finish early may wish to tackle another topic, but they will report only on their first topic chosen.)
- Use the cards as "whips." Read a card aloud and then quickly "whip" around the room, calling on students who are required to "think fast" and give a response. Students may pass, but assure them you'll be back with another sentence starter!
- Give Learning Partners (or individual students) one or both sheets and ask them to complete the sentence starters.

Student responses to any of these sentence starters can be written on a card which you have enlarged on a duplicating machine. These can then be used as class posters.

SUPPLEMENTARY ACTIVITY #7 HANDOUT #1A

Friendship Discussion Cards

You know someone is
a real friend when . . .

Something that could cause
a kid to lose a friend is . . .

Something I never do when I want
to make friends with someone is . . .

The reason some kids are
mean to other kids is . . .

Friendship Discussion Cards (continued)

Things to do to keep a friend are . . . .

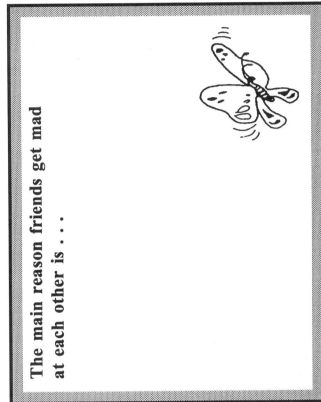

The main reason friends get mad at each other is . . . .

Kids would have more friends if only they would . . . .

The hardest thing about being a friend is . . . .

Being a Put-Downer Makes You Hard to Like

Objective
Students will learn some reasons behind put-down behavior, as well as the fact that giving put-downs can cause others not to trust them.

Students will learn techniques to help them change their put-down behaviors.

Materials
Blank transparencies and pen

Lesson 2, Transparency #1 - "How Much Does It Bug You?" (optional)

Lesson 2, Puppet Master #1, "Jesse Jackrabbit"

Lesson 2, Puppet Master #2, "Marti Mouse"

Transparency #1 - "Put-Downs Hurt Friendships"

Transparency #2 - "Why Kids Give Put-Downs—1"

Transparency #3 - "Differences Make Life More Fun"

Transparency #4 - "Why Kids Give Put-Downs—2"

Transparency #5 - "Why Kids Give Put-Downs—3"

Transparency #6 - "Kids Don't Trust a Put-Downer"

Transparency #7 - "Stop and Think: Do I REALLY Want To Be a Put-Downer?"

Transparency #8/Poster #1 - "Things You Can Do Instead—1"

Transparency #9/Poster #2 - "Things You Can Do Instead—2"

Transparency #10/Poster #3 - "Things You Can Do Instead—3"

To the Teacher
It would be a rare classroom where there was not a noticeable amount of ridicule and unfriendly comments. Many students use put-downs as an attempt to impress other students and gain status in the group. Other students may be coming from a home environment where negative feedback is the norm. Some students develop a habit of relating with others using put-downs and teasing.

Students who have developed the habit of putting down others may achieve a degree of popularity in their peer group, but it is a popularity mixed with distrust. Students who give put-downs need to find other ways of gaining attention from their peers. On the opposite side, students who are frequently targeted by others to receive put-downs often don't know how to respond to ridicule and can feel helpless and incompetent—feelings which can persist long after the ridicule has stopped. They need to learn how to respond to put-downs in order to feel comfortable in their relationships and to avoid inviting continued derision.

In this lesson students will learn some of the reasons why kids give put-downs to others—because others are different from them, because they have been treated badly themselves, or because they think giving put-downs to others makes them popular with their classmates. They will learn that put-down behavior, although it may elicit a laugh from their peers, causes others not to feel safe with or trust them. The lesson teaches students several techniques to break themselves from the habit of giving put-downs. These include using inner speech, getting their minds on something else, and choosing to have a positive interaction with a friend instead of giving a put-down.

Students who have developed the habit of relating to their peers by giving put-downs will need a great deal of encouragement and practice to change their behavior. The Supplementary Activities at the end of the lesson can provide additional practice with lesson concepts. The Supplementary Activity, "Breaking the Put-Down Habit," has scenarios for 1st, 2nd, and 3rd grades.

Lesson Presentation

REVIEW OF LESSON 2

In our last lesson we talked about some behaviors that keep kids from having friends. Can you remember what some of those behaviors were?

<table>
<tr><td>

Blank Transp. Lesson 2, Transp. #1

</td><td>

Write student responses on a blank transparency. Cue them to recall the behaviors that received the most class votes on Lesson 2, Transparency #1, "How Much Does It Bug You?" You may wish to show the transparency and point out the ones that received the most votes.

</td></tr>
</table>

PUT-DOWNS–ONE OF THE WORST BEHAVIORS

Today we're going to talk about one of the worst of the behaviors that hurts friendships. Marti Mouse and Jesse Jackrabbit are going to show you what that behavior is. Hold up your hand when you think you know.

Use the two puppets to reenact the following put-down scenario: **The class is making masks for Halloween. Jesse Jackrabbit loves art and even brought some glitter and colored yarn from home. The** class has finished their masks and are taking turns showing them to their classmates. It's Jesse's turn.

> *Jesse:* My mask is a purple sea-monster. I sprinkled the fangs with glitter so they would look shiny. The sea-monster has extra-big eyes so it can see underwater. And see this red yarn coming out of its mouth? It's a fire-breathing sea-monster! And . . .
>
> *Marti:* Give me a break! Who ever heard of a fire-breathing sea-monster? Don't you know the water would put out the monster's fire, stupid? That's the dumbest thing I ever heard of! Besides, that yarn doesn't even look like fire!

What just happened? What did Marti do that makes it hard for other kids to like him? *Call on a volunteer. Help students to recognize that Marti gave Jesse a put-down.* **How do you think Jesse felt when Marti gave him a put-down?** *Allow for student response.*

Transp. #1

Put Transparency #1, "Put-Downs Hurt Friendships," on the overhead. **A put-down is something someone says to someone else that makes the person feel bad. A put-down can be calling others a name they don't like, like "Hey, Dog Face!" or "Look out! Here comes Bigfoot!"** *Write "name-calling" on the transparency.* **Another kind of put-down is making others feel badly when they can't do something very well—laughing at their drawing or making fun of them when they miss a word in reading or strike out in baseball.** *Write "making fun of others when they can't do something very well" on the transparency.* **When you give someone a put-down, it's almost like throwing a rock at them. A rock hurts on the outside; a put-down hurts on the inside.** *Point to the rock on transparency.*

It's easy to see that kids don't want to be friends with someone who throws rocks at them. They also don't want to be friends with someone who puts them down or insults them. Today we're going to talk about why some kids like to give put-downs and how a put-downer can stop giving put-downs.

SOME PEOPLE PUT DOWN OTHERS WHO ARE DIFFERENT FROM THEM

Transp. #2

There are lots of reasons why one kid will put another kid down. Sometimes a kid will put someone else down because that person is different from them. *Put Transparency #2, "Why Kids Give Put-Downs—1," on the overhead. Point out the way the boy on the left is making fun of someone because he's different from him.* **Maybe they came from a different country or a different part of the United States and they dress differently or talk with an accent. Maybe they do things differently because of their religion or because their family has some different customs. Maybe their hair is extra curly or extra straight, or maybe they love to draw but can't seem to memorize their math facts.**

Transp. #3

What if everyone were just alike? *Put Transparency #3, "Differences Make Life More Fun," on the overhead. Discuss the fact that the kids in the picture are all just alike and they find it <u>bor-ing</u>.* **Our class would be just as BO-R-R-ING if we were all alike. We're <u>lucky</u> to have so many differences in our room.**

Just for the fun of it, let's see how many differences there are in our room. When I ask a question, raise your hand if it fits you. Remember, no putting down someone who is different from you, even if they hate something you love! *Read the following attributes, adding any that are reflected in your classroom:*

Who in this class . . .

- **Has brown eyes?**
- **Likes to eat fish?**
- **Hates baseball?**
- **Has long hair?**
- **Likes to roller skate?**
- **Has a hard time with spelling?**
- **Can draw well?**
- **Has a step-brother?**
- **Likes soccer?**

- **Is the oldest kid at your house?**

- **Has a grandma living with you?**

- **Has been to a foreign country?**

- **Has never been to Alaska?**

- **Wears black athletic shoes?**

- **Likes popcorn?**

Point to Transparency #3. **Would you rather be in a class like this, or in our class?** *Allow for student response.* **When you put someone down because they're different, you're saying you want to be in this** *(point to transparency)* **kind of class. That would be pretty boring, wouldn't it?**

SOME PUT-DOWNERS HAVE BEEN TREATED BADLY THEMSELVES

Transp. #4

There's another reason kids put other kids down. *Place Transparency #4, "Why Kids Give Put-Downs—2," on the overhead.* **Sometimes when a kid has been put down by someone, he or she will give a put-down to someone else.** *Explain the pass-the-put-down sequence on the transparency.* **When someone gives us a put-down, we get in a bad mood, don't we? When we're in a bad mood, we feel like blasting everybody in sight! Some kids have grown up in homes where people have a habit of saying mean things to each other. They feel in a bad mood a lot of the time. They've gotten into the habit of being mean because that is the way they have been treated. Sometimes when I hear somebody give a put-down, I think to myself, "I wonder if they have had their feelings hurt a lot?" How many of you have wondered the same thing?** *Ask for a show of hands.*

SOME KIDS THINK BEING A PUT-DOWNER MAKES THEM POPULAR

Transp. #5

There's another reason kids give put-downs, and I think this is the one that happens the most. Some kids just don't like themselves very much, and one way they try to feel better is by

putting other kids down. *Put Transparency #5, "Why Kids Give Put-Downs—3," on the overhead.* **Here you see two kids. The one on the left, Kid A, wants to feel bigger and more powerful than Kid B. So Kid A may pick on Kid B so he or she can feel strong.** *Point at figures on the transparency.* **Kid A may put Kid B down because Kid A thinks he or she will be more popular with the other kids. Put-downers think that if they can get other kids to laugh at their put-downs, the other kids will like them more. When you hear one kid putting down another kid, how do you feel about it? Does it make you like them more?** *Allow for student input.* **When a put-downer picks on somebody, do you think, "Wow! That put-downer is really a neat kid!"** *Allow for student response.*

KIDS DON'T REALLY TRUST A PUT-DOWNER

Transp. #6

A put-downer wants <u>really</u> <u>badly</u> to be noticed and liked. But do you know what is sad about a put-downer? *Put Transparency #6, "Kids Don't Trust a Put-Downer," on the overhead.* **Kids don't really <u>trust</u> a put-downer. They may laugh at the put-down, but on the inside they don't really trust the put-downer—for all they know, they may be the next one to be insulted by the put-downer!** *Read and explain the cartoon on the transparency.*

Transp. #7

I think everyone in our class wants to have friends and be liked. But none of us is perfect, and put-downs slip out from time to time. If you find yourself giving other kids put-downs, you need to STOP and THINK. *Put Transparency #7, "Stop and Think: Do I REALLY Want To Be a Put-Downer?," on the overhead.* **Do I want everyone to see that I'm mean? Is it worth it to get a few laughs at my put-down if people don't trust me?**

TRICKS THAT CAN HELP A PUT-DOWNER STOP GIVING PUT-DOWNS

Transp. #8

Maybe you have just gotten into the habit of giving put-downs, but you don't really want to be a put-downer. If you don't <u>want</u> to be a put-downer, there are some things you can do to help yourself stop giving put-downs. The first thing you can do is to <u>talk to yourself</u>. *Put Transparency #8, "Things You Can Do Instead—*

1," on the overhead, covering the words, "Different is O.K.," and "Put-downers are hard to like."*

You can ask yourself how it would feel if someone were to give a put-down to you.

Uncover "Different is O.K." **You can remind yourself that "Different is O.K." Remember that you wouldn't really like it if everyone was exactly alike.**

Uncover "Put-downers are hard to like." **You can remember that put-downers are hard to like. Remind yourself that you don't want everyone to think of you as mean and a bully who picks on people.**

Transp. #9	**There's another thing you can do to stop yourself from giving a put-down.** *Put Transparency #9, "Things You Can Do Instead—2," on the overhead.* **This put-downer <u>really</u> wants to ask this kid if he just stepped off a spaceship from Mars, but he doesn't want to be a put-downer. So he's going to <u>get his mind on something else</u>. He's decided to go talk to a friend. He could have decided to finish his spelling or go get a drink of water. Can you think of some things he could do instead of giving a put-down? How could he get his mind on something else?** *Allow students to brainstorm ways the put-downer could take his mind off giving a put-down.*

Transp. #10	**Good! Those are some great ways of stopping yourself from giving a put-down! Here's one more trick you can use when you feel like giving a put-down.** *Put Transparency #10, "Things You Can Do Instead—3," on the overhead.* **Here's a put-downer who wants to stop giving put-downs. She's thinking of a put-down.** *Read "Nat! The brat! You're so fat!" from the transparency.* **This put-downer has decided to use the "Turn-Yourself-Inside-Out" Trick. She's going to turn herself "inside out." Instead of being someone who wants to say something mean to someone she doesn't like, she's going to change herself into someone who says something nice to someone she <u>does</u> like.**

To do this, she doesn't just make something up. She thinks of someone she likes and makes a friendly comment about something they have done or are wearing. This trick works just like magic! Instead of feeling like a put-downer, she feels like a

friend! What are some positive things you could say to a friend? *Allow for student response. Help them think of compliments on clothing or appearance, classwork, something done well during P.E., a good grade on a test, etc.*

PRACTICING THINGS TO DO INSTEAD OF GIVING PUT-DOWNS

Transp. #8
Transp. #9
Transp. #10

Good job! Let's practice with the Marti Mouse and Jesse Jackrabbit puppets. Let's pretend we're going to help Marti break the put-down habit. I'll read to you about a time Marti felt like giving Jesse a put-down. The person operating the Marti puppet will help Marti stop being a put-downer by using one of the techniques we've talked about. *Put Transparencies #8, #9, and #10 on the overhead as you review each of the three techniques.* **Marti can either <u>talk to himself</u>** *(Transparency #8),* **get his mind on something else** *(Transparency #9),* **or use the Turn-Yourself-Inside-Out Trick** *(Transparency #10).*

Let me show you what I mean. *Put both puppets on your hands and read the following scenario, moving the puppets to indicate which puppet students should focus on as you read.* **Jesse has just come in the classroom door. She's wearing a jacket that's much too big for her. It's probably an old one of her sister's. A put-down pops into Marti's mind. He wants to say, "Hey, Jesse! Are you going camping? I like your tent!" But Marti thinks, "Do I <u>really</u> want to be a put-downer?"**

Can anyone help Marti do something else instead of giving a put-down? Can you help Marti use the three techniques we've just learned? *Call on student volunteers to suggest ways Marti can talk to himself, get his mind on something else, or use the Turn-Yourself-Inside-Out Trick.*

Read the following scenarios or some of your own to the class, calling on student volunteers to help the Marti puppet change his put-down habit using the three techniques just taught. (In order to get the greatest amount of practice from this exercise, ask for examples of each of the three techniques for each scenario whenever appropriate.) If students are confident enough, you may wish to allow volunteers to operate the two puppets and have the Marti puppeteer choose and act out alternative behaviors for Marti.

SCENARIO I

The teacher has just handed back yesterday's math assignment. Jesse, who isn't very good at math, is happy with her grade—a C+. Marti, who is good at math, got an A. A put-down pops into Marti's mind! He wants to say to Jesse, "What are you so happy about? I got an <u>A</u>!" But then he thinks, "Do I <u>really</u> want to be a put-downer?" What can Marti do instead?

SCENARIO II

Marti and a group of other kids are getting ready to play kickball at recess. Jesse comes up to the group and asks if she can play. A put-down pops into Marti's mind! He wants to say to Jesse, "Jesse, you've got two left feet. Go play dolls instead!" But then Marti thinks, "Do I <u>really</u> want to be a put-downer?" What can Marti do instead of saying the put-down?

SCENARIO III

Jesse is a very good artist. She's just finished a picture for her science project and asks Marti, "How do you like my picture?" Marti is having trouble with his picture, and a put-down pops into his mind! He starts to say, "Jesse, you think you're the best artist in the school, don't you? Big deal!" But then Marti thinks, "Do I <u>really</u> want to be a put-downer?" Can you help Marti do something else to break the put-down habit?

SCENARIO IV

When all the kids are getting off the school bus, Jesse slips on the steps and falls to the ground. She isn't hurt but she is embarrassed. A put-down pops into Marti's mind! He wants to say, "Is that what you learned in dancing class, Jesse?" But then Marti thinks, "Do I <u>really</u> want to be a put-downer?" What can Marti do instead to stop himself from being a put-downer?

SCENARIO V

Marti is sitting across the lunch table from Jesse, who is eating a very juicy sandwich. Mayonnaise is running down her fingers and a piece of tomato drops out onto the table. A put-down pops into Marti's mind! He wants to say, "Is that a good sandwich, Jesse? Oink! Oink!" Then he thinks, "Do I <u>really</u> want to be a put-downer?" What can Marti do to break the put-down habit?

SCENARIO VI

Marti and Jesse are asked to take some books back to the library. Marti is in a hurry to get back to the classroom and take his turn on the computer. Jesse is having a hard time keeping up with Marti, and she drops her armful of books on the hall floor. A put-down pops into Marti's mind! He wants to say, "Nice going, Jesse! You're really a prize-winning klutz!" But then he thinks, "Do I <u>really</u> want to be a put-downer?" Can you help Marti do something else instead?

SCENARIO VII

Jesse comes into the classroom just before the bell rings and slips quietly into her seat. She has a new haircut, and it is kind of funny-looking. You can tell by looking at Jesse's face that she doesn't like it much. Marti takes one look at Jesse's hair, and a put-down pops into his mind! He wants to say loudly so everyone will hear, "Hey Jesse! It looks like you had a fight with the scissors, and the scissors won!" Then he thinks, "Do I <u>really</u> want to be a put-downer?" Can you help Marti break the put-down habit?

SCENARIO VIII

Jesse is making a poster for social studies; she has all her marking pens spread out around her. Marti's red marker is all dried up, and he asks Jesse if he could use hers. She says no! A put-down pops into Marti's mind! He wants to say, "O.K. for you, you selfish pig! Just see if I ever let you use any of my stuff!" But then he thinks, "Do I <u>really</u> want to be a put-downer—even if she deserves it?" What can Marti do to keep from being a put-downer?

After Scenario VIII, you may wish to point out to students that, even if the other person seems to deserve a put-down, they don't want to let that person's poor behavior trick them into being a put-downer.

IT'S HARD TO BREAK THE PUT-DOWN HABIT

You've done a very good job helping Marti break the put-down habit. Even though some of his put-downs are funny, he's decided he doesn't want to be a put-downer just to get a laugh. Giving put-downs is a hard habit to break, and Marti will need to practice these techniques to change it.

Poster #1
Poster #2
Poster #3

We'll need to practice, too. During this week let's try really hard to kick the put-down habit. I'll put these posters up to help us remember things we can do instead of giving put-downs. *Show them Posters #1, #2, and #3 ("Things You Can Do Instead").* **If you're able to stop yourself from giving a put-down by using one of these techniques this week, I'd like for you to come up and whisper it in my ear. I want to be the first one to congratulate you!**

LESSON REVIEW

Review the lesson asking students to tell you what they've learned. To help reinforce the concepts of this lesson, you may wish to hang up the poster "Don't give put-downs." (Poster #10, Appendix D).

Use the Supplementary Activities to provide additional practice of the skills taught in this lesson.

TRANSPARENCY #1

Put-Downs Hurt Friendships

TRANSPARENCY #2

Why Kids Give Put-Downs

1.

Because someone is different from them.

Differences Make Life More Fun

Why Kids Give Put-Downs

2.
Because they got one.

TRANSPARENCY #5

Why Kids Give Put-Downs

> ## 3.
> *To try and look big or impress other kids.*

Kid A   Kid B

Kids Don't Trust a Put-Downer

TRANSPARENCY #7

Stop and Think:
"Do I REALLY Want To Be a Put-Downer?"

TRANSPARENCY #8/POSTER #1

Things You Can Do Instead

1.
Talk to yourself.

TRANSPARENCY #9/POSTER #2

Things You Can Do Instead

2.

Get your mind onto something else.

Things You Can Do Instead

3.
Use the "Turn-Yourself-Inside-Out" Trick.

Breaking the Put-Down Habit

Objective   Students will practice choosing one of the three techniques taught in the lesson to break the habit of giving put-downs.

Materials   Lesson 2, Puppet Master #2, "Marti Mouse"

"Scenarios" (Supplementary Activity Materials Sheet #1A-#1B, #2A-#2B, or #3A-#3B)

Posters #1, #2, and #3 ("Things You Can Do Instead") from lesson

Procedure   The same procedure can be used for 1st, 2nd, and 3rd graders. Put the Marti Mouse puppet on your hand. Read one of the following scenarios for your grade level or make up examples of your own. Then move around the room calling on students to help Marti choose one of the behavior techniques from the lesson (talk to yourself, get your mind on something else, or use the Turn-Yourself-Inside-Out Trick) in order to break the put-down habit. Ask students to give examples of the alternative behavior, such as: asking yourself "How would it feel?" (talk to yourself); going to the water fountain to get a drink (get your mind on something else); or complimenting a friend on their new haircut (Turn-Yourself-Inside-Out Trick). Move quickly from student to student, telling those who don't offer a response that you'll be back to them later. Remind students to refer to the three posters for ideas.

VARIATION

After you have read a scenario and called on a student to respond, specify which of the three techniques you want them to use in helping Marti to do something else instead of giving a put-down.

SUPPLEMENTARY ACTIVITY MATERIALS SHEET #1A

Scenarios
for First Grade

SCENARIO I

Marti is drawing a picture with his crayons. He gets up to get a drink, and when he comes back to his desk, the girl next to him is using his blue crayon. He feels like saying in an angry voice, "Quit taking my crayons, Birdbrain!"

SCENARIO II

Marti and a friend are playing checkers. Marti has won four games and the friend has won only one. Marti wins again, and the friend says he doesn't want to play anymore. Marti feels like saying, "Don't be such a bad sport! You're just mad because you lost again!"

SCENARIO III

Some of the girls are playing jump rope at recess, and Marti wants to see if he can jump Hot Pepper. The girls won't let him have a turn, and Marti feels like telling the girls, "Who wants to jump rope with a bunch of dumb girls anyway!"

SCENARIO IV

A boy in Marti's class is having trouble learning his math facts. Marti thinks it would be funny to make him mad by calling him "Mr. Math."

SCENARIO V

Marti and a girl in his class are straightening the book shelf for the teacher. The girl is very bossy about it and wants to put the books on the shelf just so. Marti wants to get the job done so he can take his turn on the computer. When the girl starts telling him how to do it, Marti feels like saying, "Do it yourself, Miss Priss! I'm outta here!"

SCENARIO VI

Marti's teacher reads to the class every day after lunch. Sometimes the kids in the class bring a book they like for her to read. A girl in Marti's class brings a book and asks the teacher to read it to the class. Marti thinks the book is a girls' book and he feels like saying in a loud voice, "Don't read that book! It's dumb!"

Scenarios
for First Grade (continued)

SCENARIO VII

A girl in Marti's class brought her favorite coloring book to school to show to the class for show-and-tell. While she's showing it, Marti feels like saying, "My cat can color better than that!"

SCENARIO VIII

There's a new girl in Marti's class. She wears clothes that are old and too big for her. Marti thinks it would be funny to call her "Bag Lady."

SCENARIO IX

There's a boy in Marti's class who is small for his age. He can't run very fast and isn't good at sports. The teacher is dividing the class into teams for relay races, and the small kid is supposed to be on Marti's team. Marti feels like complaining, "No way! He's a loser!"

SCENARIO X

Everyone in Marti's class has a reading book to take home and practice reading. One of the girls has trouble reading and the teacher gave her a very easy book. When Marti sees her book, he feels like saying, "That's a baby book!"

SUPPLEMENTARY ACTIVITY MATERIALS SHEET #2A

Scenarios
for Second Grade

SCENARIO I

Marti's class has a new student. The boy is from a foreign country. He wears his hair in an odd style and speaks with an accent. Marti feels like copying the funny way he talks and making the rest of the kids laugh.

SCENARIO II

Marti stayed up late last night finishing his math homework. When the time comes to hand it in, the girl behind him, who is a math whiz, doesn't have her homework finished! Marti is delighted! He wants to say, "Hey, everybody, the Math Genius just got a zero on her homework!"

SCENARIO III

One of the kids in Marti's neighborhood just got kicked off the soccer team for missing too many practices. Marti never liked the kid much, and he wants to say, "Good! Maybe we can win some games now!"

SCENARIO IV

Marti's little brother has been a real pest all evening. Finally his mother gets fed up and puts him to bed early. At last Marti will be able to finish his homework in peace. Marti feels like saying, "Good night, Brat!"

SCENARIO V

A girl in Marti's class spends a lot of time combing her hair, filing her nails, and looking at herself in the mirror. Marti feels like telling her no one likes her because she's so stuck on herself.

SCENARIO VI

It's Saturday and Marti and his friends are trying to play a game of softball in the vacant lot. A little kid from down the street keeps hanging around, chasing the ball when they miss it, and pestering them to let him play. Marti feels like saying, "Sure! You can play. You can be first base!"

Scenarios
for Second Grade (continued)

SCENARIO VII

There's a boy in Marti's class who is small for his age and can't play sports very well. He can't kick a soccer ball, always strikes out, and is too fat to fun very fast. When the kid is assigned to Marti's kickball team, Marti starts to say, "No fair! If he's going to be on our team, we might as well say we lost and save ourselves the trouble!"

SCENARIO VIII

There's a girl in Marti's class who is always wanting to help the teacher. She asks if she can hand out papers; she is always the first to raise her hand to run an errand; sometimes she even stays after school to help the teacher straighten up the room. Marti has started calling her Teacher's Pet. He feels like calling her that right now.

SCENARIO IX

Marti is reading his science report to the class. He copied it out of the encyclopedia and some of the words are strange to him. He isn't doing a very good job of reading the report and stumbles over a big word. A kid in the back of the room snickers. Marti feels like saying to the kid, "Shut up, Jerk Face! At least I don't have bad breath!"

SCENARIO X

Marti and a girl in his class are making a bulletin board about Earth Day for the class. They're putting up pictures of different animals that are in danger of becoming extinct. The girl keeps putting the pictures up crooked. Marti feels like telling her his little brother could do a better job than she's doing.

Scenarios
for Third Grade

SCENARIO I
There's a boy in Marti's class who is bigger than everyone else. Marti thinks it would be funny to call him the Incredible Hulk.

SCENARIO II
Marti and his mother had an argument before school this morning and Marti is in a bad mood. When a boy in his class asks if he can borrow a pencil, Marti feels like saying, "Get off the planet, you moocher!"

SCENARIO IIII
Marti is waiting at the bus stop with some of his friends. A little kid walks up to the bus stop; he's wearing thick glasses. Marti knows his friends would laugh if he said, "Hey kid, are those glasses or goggles?"

SCENARIO IV
Marti's teen-aged sister is getting dressed for a date. She's wearing a shirt she made in her home economics class at high school. Marti thinks it would be funny to say, "Gosh, Sis, I thought Halloween was still two months away!"

SCENARIO V
A kid in Marti's class got a new game for his birthday. He is trying to get some of the other kids to play it with him. Marti thinks it's a boring game, and he feels like saying, "Why don't you get a kindergartner to play with you? That's a baby game!"

SCENARIO VI
A girl in Marti's class has a new pair of athletic shoes. She says her mother got them on sale. Marti's sister had a pair just like them last year, and he thinks of saying, "Those shoes are last year's style!"

SCENARIO VII
A kid in Marti's neighborhood has been building a model car. He's been bragging about it for two weeks. When the model is finished, the kid brings it over to Marti's house. The glue is dried in globs and the decals are stuck on crooked. Marti feels like saying to the kid, "My little brother could have done a better job than that!"

SUPPLEMENTARY ACTIVITY MATERIALS SHEET #3B

Scenarios
for Third Grade (continued)

SCENARIO VIII

Marti's class is playing softball. Marti is playing first base for his team. A girl on the other team hit the ball and is racing for first base. Marti tags her out, and she starts to cry, saying that Marti hit her too hard with the ball. Marti thinks she's being a bad sport and feels like saying, "Don't be such a crybaby! You're just mad because I got you out!"

SCENARIO IX

It's the first day of school and Marti is talking to a couple of friends about his summer vacation. This other kid keeps interrupting and telling about what he did during the summer. Marti wants to say, "Butt out, Blabbermouth. Nobody cares!"

SCENARIO X

A boy in Marti's neighborhood is on the baseball team at the YMCA. His team has new hats, and he wears his everywhere. Marti is tired of hearing about basketball and feels like saying, "You look like somebody on Mr. Rogers' Neighborhood in that hat!

The Secret to Making Friends: Make Others Feel Special

Objective   Students will learn specific behaviors that promote friendship.

Materials   Blank transparency and pens

Lesson 2, Puppet Master #1, "Jesse Jackrabbit"

Lesson 2, Puppet Master #2, "Marti Mouse"

Transparency #1 - "What's the Secret of Friendship?"

Handout #1 - "The Secret to Making a Friend"

Transparency #2 - "Different Kinds of Friends"

Transparency #3 - "I Felt SPECIAL When . . ."

Transparency #4/Handout #2 - "20 Ways You Can Make Others Feel Special"

Transparency #5/Handout #3 - "Sharing"

Posters - All posters in Appendix D

To the Teacher   Children who know how to be attentive, helpful and approving gain peer acceptance and score high on sociometric measures. Low sociometric status, or being unpopular, is largely a function of a lack of these skills. By teaching students behaviors like sharing, taking turns, playing fair, and complimenting, you can help them increase their chances for friendship.

Because the friendship skills of giving and receiving compliments are so important, these skills are the focus of Lessons 6 and 7.

This lesson first attempts to help students make the distinction between an acquaintance, a playmate, and a best friend. This helps students set realistic expectations regarding how much attention and support they receive from others.

The lesson then introduces the maxim "To have friends you have to make them feel special." Students are given a list of 20 ways to make a person feel special. The lesson provides opportunities for students to practice a number of these prosocial behaviors.

The Supplementary Activities that follow the lesson can be used to extend the learning and provide more practice with lesson concepts. You may even prefer some of these activities to those used the lesson. If so, substitute them or add them to the lesson.

In Appendix D you'll find the posters identified in the materials section. Displaying them will remind students of the lesson concepts. You may decide to hang up all the posters at once, or you may display a different poster each day to focus on a specific behavior everyone in the class will try to do.

If your school uses a grade-leveled approach to this curriculum, the lesson itself can be taught each year as the concepts bear repeating. Students bring a new awareness level, new abilities to process, and new examples to each lesson. Use the following activities at these suggested grade levels. Some first grade activities can't be used until mid-year. Students can work in pairs and help each other with the reading.

1st "Guess Who the Animal Friends Are!"
(Supplementary Activity #1)
"Hats Off to Friendship!"
(Supplementary Activity #2)

2nd "The Friendship Flipper"
(Supplementary Activity #3)
"Kids' Kindness Laws"
(Supplementary Activity #4)

3rd "How I Treat My Friends"
(Supplementary Activity #5)
"Making a Circle of Friends"
(Supplementary Activity #6)

You may also want to read or make available to students some of the following books on sharing, one of the friendship behaviors emphasized in this lesson:

Brenner, B. . . . . *Mr. Tall and Mrs. Small*
Cole, W. . . . . *Aunt Bella's Umbrella*
Consall, B. . . . . *It's Mine*
Ginsburg, M. . . . . *Mushroom in the Rain*
Keats, E.J. . . . . *Peter's Chair*
Lionni, L. . . . . *Frederick*
Scott, A.H. . . . . *On Mother's Lap*
Silverstein, S. . . . . *The Giving Tree*
Steig, W. . . . . *Amos and Boris*
Steptoe, J. . . . . *Stevie*
Zolotow, C. . . . . *Do You Know What I'll Do?*

Lesson Presentation

REVIEW OF LESSONS 2 AND 3

In our last two lessons we've focused on the behaviors that keep people from being friends and we learned why kids who give put-downs are hard to like. *Review previous concepts as you think appropriate.*

THE SECRET TO FRIENDSHIP

**Transp. #1
Handout #1**

Today we're going to talk about things to do that will make you easy to like. We're going to learn the secret of making friends. *Show Transparency #1, "What's the Secret of Friendship?" Ask some students to volunteer their guesses as to what they think the secret of friendship is. Write their responses around the figures on the transparency. Then give students Handout #1, "The Secret to Making a Friend." Read them the directions and ask them not to say the answer until you call time. When you call time, all the students who know the answer can say it out loud together. Say:* **"Making someone feel special" sums up all the nice things a friend does. You could also say a friend is someone who makes you feel good.**

ACQUAINTANCES, PLAYMATES, AND BEST FRIENDS

Transp. #2

Let's take a look at the different kinds of friends we can have. *Show Transparency #2, "Different Kinds of Friends."* One kind of friend is an <u>acquaintance</u>. This is a person we only play with now and then. We usually don't do too many things to make an acquaintance feel special. Another kind of friend is called a <u>playmate</u>, or a regular friend. Playmates are kids who play with each other quite a bit. They usually do some things to make each other feel special. The next kind of friend is called a <u>best friend</u>. Best friends play together as often as they can and do a lot of things to make each other feel special.

Some kids think that everyone they know is their best friend. It's really only possible to have one or two people for a best friend at a time. Why do you think this is true? *Allow for student responses.* Since best friends like to be together a lot and should do many things to make each other feel special, most people only have <u>time</u> for one or two best friends. But you can still have several regular friends and lots of acquaintances.

WAYS THAT SOMEONE HAS MADE YOU FEEL SPECIAL

Transp. #3

People make best friends or regular friends by doing things that make each other feel special. Here are some things that kids have said their friends did that made them feel special: *Show Transparency #3, "I Felt SPECIAL When . . . ." Read some of the examples and ask students to think of a time when someone treated them in a way that made them feel good or special. Write some of the student responses on the transparency.*

WAYS YOU COULD MAKE SOMEONE FEEL SPECIAL

Blank Transp.
Transp. #4
Handout #2

Now put a blank transparency on the overhead. Ask students to brainstorm things that they could do to make someone feel special and thereby build a friendship. Put Transparency #4, "20 Ways You Can Make Others Feel Special," on the overhead and give students a handout of the same (Handout #2). Read the list to students. As you do so, tell students to put a star by the items on the list that are different from the ones they just brainstormed. Have them underline the behaviors they feel they already do a lot of the time. As each behavior is mentioned, discuss how inappropriate it is to do the opposite.

PRACTICING MAKING OTHERS FEEL SPECIAL THROUGH ROLE-PLAY

As you can see, there are lots of ways to be nice to others so that they'll feel special. Usually when you are nice to people, they are nice back and are more likely to want to be your friend. Let me show you what I mean. I've got some ideas for situations we can act out using some of the ways we've just learned to make others feel special.

One way to make a friend feel special is to be interested in what they're saying and to listen to them instead of interrupting. Let's pretend that one of you just got back from a hiking trip and you're telling a few of us about it. You saw a mother deer and its fawn. Let's say that I went hiking last year and I saw a bear! I'm dying to mention it, but I want you to feel special—so I'm not going to interrupt you. Who would like to volunteer to be the person telling about their hiking trip and seeing the deer? *Pick a loquacious volunteer. Model listening attentively, drawing the person out, and waiting for an appropriate time to share your story.* So, as you can see, listening to someone and not interrupting is a good way to make a person feel special.

Puppets

To make others feel special, you just have to decide to be nice, and then practice a little so what you do will look natural. Let's do some practicing now. *Use the Jesse and Marti puppets from Lesson 2, or use your own puppets.* Let's pretend that Jesse and Marti are kids you want to be friends with. I'll tell you a situation where you could choose to be nice in a way that would make Jesse or Marti want to be friends with you. After I read the situation, raise your hand if you can think of a way to make Jesse or Marti feel special.

Read each of the following scenarios, using the specified puppet to play the role of the person who is to be made to feel special. Ad lib lines as necessary for the puppet to say which fit the scenario. Call on student volunteers to suggest appropriate responses. Have the students with the best suggestions say their response to the puppet. Take the puppet over to the volunteer's desk or have the student walk up to the puppet.

If students don't volunteer enough appropriate responses, model some friendly responses by speaking to the puppet yourself. For some scenarios you may wish to start by modeling a response and then asking students to provide other responses.

OFFER TO DO A FAVOR

You and Jesse are running to the school office at lunch recess because she needs to call her mom. Just as you get to the office door, Jesse remembers she left her jacket out on the playfield. How could you make Jesse feel special?

LET THE OTHER PERSON GO FIRST

You and Marti have both been allowed some free time because you finished your work early. The teacher says you can go back to one of the centers where there are lots of art materials, games, and other fun things to do. How could you make Marti feel special?

STICK UP FOR SOMEONE

You see Marti on the playfield. Marti is being picked on by some other kids. When the playground teacher comes over and asks what's going on, the other kids blame it on Marti and say he started it. You know that isn't true. What could you do to help make Marti feel special?

LET SOMEONE KNOW WHEN YOU LIKE THEIR IDEAS

Jesse got the idea that it would be fun to start a club for kids that like horses. She thought that club members could loan each other books about horses and show each other their drawings and models of horses. You think that this is a great idea! What could you do to help Jesse feel special?

BE HONEST

You and Marti are playing in Marti's room at his home. Marti goes to the kitchen to get you both a snack. While he's gone, you pick up one of the model planes he has made. You accidentally drop the plane and one of the wings comes off! You can kind of put it together again, but it's really still broken. You hear Marti coming back to the room. You could show Marti you think he's special by being honest with him. What would you say?

ENCOURAGE SOMEONE WHO LOOKS DISCOURAGED

Marti is really feeling bad! Right at the end of his soccer game he had a clear shot to make a goal and he missed it. If he had made the goal his team would have won—instead, they lost the game. What could you say to show Marti you think he's special?

LET YOUR FRIENDS HAVE OTHER FRIENDS

You and Jesse haven't known each other for long, but you really like her and you have fun when the two of you play together. During the last recess Jesse didn't play with you. Instead, she played with one of her other friends. What could you say to Jesse to show her that you are her friend even when she plays with someone else?

SHARE WITH SOMEONE

You and Jesse are at recess. You finally got the place on the parallel bars you like best. You've been waiting your turn all recess and now there's only a few minutes of recess left. Jesse is next in line. What could you do to make Jesse feel special?

TAKING A CLOSER LOOK AT SHARING

After students have finished discussing the last role play, say: **Sometimes you send the most important message not by what you say to your friends but by how you treat them. The saying "Actions speak louder than words" is true in friendship. Sharing things is an action that really helps kids have friends.**

**Transp. #5
Handout #3**

Let's talk some more about sharing things. Sometimes it's not so hard to share things; other times it can be really tough. *Give students Handout #3, "Sharing," and show them the corresponding transparency (Transparency #5). Read the sentence starters on the hand-out/transparency to students and give them a few minutes to complete them. Discuss each sentence starter, having students share their responses. Now, pose the following dilemma:*

Let's pretend that you're eating a snack. There are a lot of kids around you. One kid asks you to share some of your snack with him or her. You know if you share some with this kid, the other kids are all going to ask you for some, too. You don't want to be selfish, but you don't want to lose your whole snack, either! What could you do in a situation like this? *Allow for student responses. You may wish to suggest the following solutions if students don't think of them. Say:*

1. **Explain the situation to the person who is asking:**

   - "If I give you one, everyone else will want one, too."

   - "There just aren't enough to go around."

   - "If it was just you and me, I'd share, but there are too many people around for everyone to have some."

2. **Offer to share at a different time:**

   - "I'd like to share with you, but how about another time?"

   - "I've got my heart set on this treat."

   - "I'd feel bad if I gave you some and not the others."

   - "How about if I save some for you to have later when we're alone?"

Let's try another example of a time when it's hard to know what to do about sharing. Let's pretend that the teacher told your class that on Friday everyone would be making things out of clay. You promised your mother you would make her something she said she would like, a clay bird's nest with eggs. When you get your clay, there's just enough brown clay left for you to make the nest. As you are working on your nest, a kid you'd like to be friends with comes over to you. This kid is making a log cabin out of brown clay and needs a piece just about the size you have to finish the cabin. What should you do? *Allow for student responses.*

Most of the time sharing isn't this complicated. You'll probably find that sharing is one of the best ways to make and keep a friend. Kids tend to like other kids who share. Nobody likes a selfish person.

When you decide to share a toy or something else and there's only that one to play with, it can be hard to wait. What can you do when you're waiting so that the time doesn't seem so long until it's your turn again? *Allow for student response. Summarize the discussion by suggesting that a person can:*

1. **Set a specific time period for each person to use the toy or equipment.**

2. **Do some other activity while they're waiting.**

3. **Play with a different toy.**

4. **Read or draw to make the time go faster.**

5. **Think about something interesting that gets their mind off of the thing they're waiting for.**

Sharing is hard sometimes, but it's worth it because no one likes a selfish person.

LESSON REVIEW

Review the lesson by asking students to try to remember the secret to making a friend, which they discovered in the code sheet they did at the beginning of the lesson. Have them tell their Learning Partner the secret. Give them the answer—"Make others feel special!"—and have those students whose partners said the correct answer raise their hands. Continue the lesson review by doing a "whip" around the room, asking students to respond to one of these sentence stems:

- *I learned . . . .*

- *I was surprised that . . . .*

- *What I'll remember most is . . . .*

Work for the transfer of the concepts of this lesson to students' everyday lives by asking students to each think of a time today or tomorrow when they will do something to make someone feel special. You may wish to suggest a specific behavior or behaviors. Have the students decide what they will do and then take a moment to imagine themselves doing it.

Use the Supplementary Activities to provide additional practice with lesson skills and concepts. Students particularly like the "Friendship Flipper" which provides opportunities for pro-social behavior.

What's the Secret of Friendship?

HANDOUT #1

The Secret to Making a Friend

Directions:

Color in only those letters that have a *, then read the secret message about how to make and keep friends!

The secret to making a friend is to:

__ __ __ __   __ __ __   __ __ __ __ __

__ __ __ __   __ __ __ __ __ __ __ __!

Different Kinds of Friends

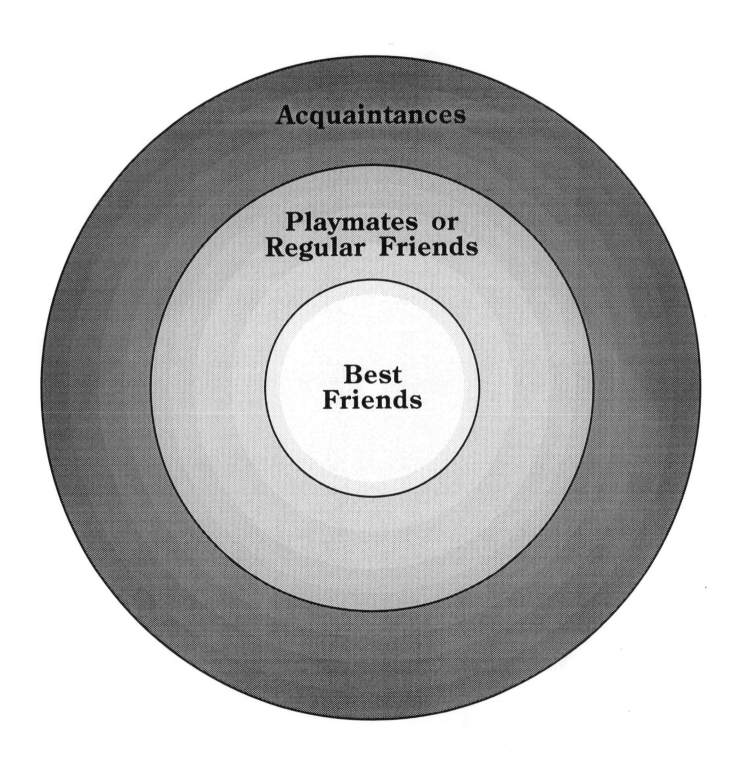

Acquaintances

Playmates or
Regular Friends

Best
Friends

I Felt SPECIAL When . . .

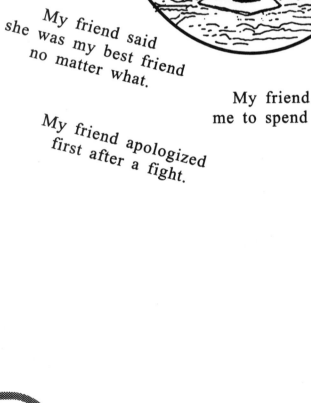

"Thanks to your home run, we won the game!"

My friend taught me how to roller skate.

My friend stuck up for me.

My friend said "Cool Idea!" to me.

My friend told people that I was good in math.

My friend gave me a net and a bug case for my birthday.

My friend said she'd always wait for me.

My friend said she was my best friend no matter what.

My friend said "Wow!" after she watched me in gymnastics.

My friend invited me to spend the night.

My friend apologized first after a fight.

20 Ways You Can Make Others Feel Special

_____ **1.** Ask them to play with you.

_____ **2.** Ask them what they would like to play.

_____ **3.** Let them know when you like their ideas.

_____ **4.** Let them go first.

_____ **5.** Play fair.

_____ **6.** Be a good sport.

_____ **7.** Offer to share things with them.

_____ **8.** Offer to help them with things.

_____ **9.** Offer to let them borrow something.

_____ **10.** Be honest with them.

_____ **11.** Help them feel better when they make mistakes.

_____ **12.** Stick up for them.

_____ **13.** Offer to do them a favor.

_____ **14.** Listen to them.

_____ **15.** Encourage them when they try new things.

_____ **16.** Give them compliments.

_____ **17.** Keep secrets and promises.

_____ **18.** Apologize if you hurt their feelings.

_____ **19.** Forgive them if they do something wrong.

_____ **20.** Let them have other friends.

Sharing

Something I like to share is _____.

Something I don't like to share with anyone is _____

_____.

One thing I could share more often is _____

_____.

Something I wish a friend would share with me is _____

_____.

**Something I could say to make it easier for someone to share
things with me is** _____

_____.

"Would you like some of my snack?"

Guess Who the Animal Friends Are!

Objective   Students will focus on behaviors that make others feel special.

Materials   Supplementary Activity #1 Handout, "Animal Friends," for each student

Supplementary Activity #1 Transparency, "Animal Friends" (optional)

Crayons for each student

Procedure   Give each student a copy of the handout, "Animal Friends." Tell them the animals are learning how to make each other feel special. Read each of the following riddles and have students guess which animal is making a friend feel special. Have students color that animal the color designated in the riddle.

After completing the six riddles, several animals will not yet be colored in. You may have the children color the rest of the animals or, if appropriate in your classroom, ask student volunteers to make up riddles of their own for the remaining animals until they are all colored.

Use the activity to stimulate discussion about ways they can make someone feel special in their class or family.

THE RIDDLES
Eloise Elephant's peanut rolled down a hole. Her trunk wasn't long enough to reach it. GUESS WHO slithered on his belly right down the hole and got the peanut for Eloise! Color him green. **(Sassafras S. Snake)**
Gus Gorilla was flying his new kite. A strong gust of wind suddenly blew it into a tall tree. Gus was too big to climb out on the small branches where his kite was stuck. GUESS WHO stretched her neck way, way up and got Gus's kite for him! Color her orange. **(Greta Giraffe)**
When it began to snow, Lorna Lizard was cold! "I don't have any fur to keep me warm," Lorna said with chattering teeth. GUESS WHO made Lorna a fuzzy wool sweater to keep her warm! Color him tan or white. **(Sheldon Sheep)**

Wally Wolf was unhappy. The ants had moved into his cupboard and were eating him out of house and home. "What am I going to do?" Wally moaned. GUESS WHO came over and got rid of the ants for Wally! Color her brown.

(Anna Maria Anteater)

Marvella Mouse was so hungry! She hadn't eaten for two days, and she had three baby mice to feed. GUESS WHO gave her half of his banana! Color him black. **(Mortimer Monkey)**

Teddy Toucan was trying to pull a nice juicy worm out of the ground, but his beak was too large and clumsy. GUESS WHO carefully pecked the worm out of the ground for Teddy! Color her red.

(Henrietta Hen)

Animal Friends

SUPPLEMENTARY ACTIVITY #2

Hats Off to Friendship!

Directions:

Color the hats that name things **YOU** do to make others feel special.

Ask kids to play with you.

Apologize when it was your fault.

Play fair.

Let others go first.

Let others decide what to play.

Share things.

The Friendship Flipper

Directions:

Use the Friendship Flipper to decide what friendship behavior you will do today! Follow the steps below to fold and use the Flipper.

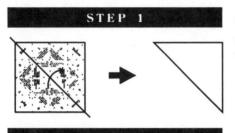

STEP 1

Cut out the Flipper along the dark black line and **fold** the Flipper in half, making a big triangle with the writing inside.

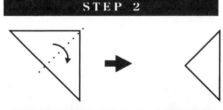

STEP 2

Fold this triangle in half to make a smaller triangle. **Crease** the edges well.

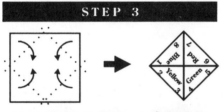

STEP 3

Unfold the Flipper. **Turn** the Flipper over so that the blank side is up. **Fold** each of the four corners in to the very center of the square. Now your Flipper will look like the sample.

STEP 4

Turn the Flipper over, and **fold** each of the new corners in to the center again. **Crease** all the edges well! Your Flipper will now look like the sample.

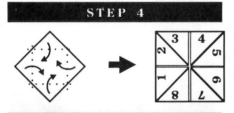

STEP 5

Fold the Flipper in half so only the names of the colors show.

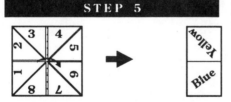

STEP 6

Fold the Flipper in half one more time so that it is one small square.

STEP 7

Unfold the last two folds, so the Flipper looks like it did in step #5.

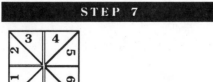

SUPPLEMENTARY ACTIVITY #3 HANDOUT #1

To Work the Friendship Flipper

1. Stick your left thumb in the Red pocket and your two fingers next to it in the Blue pocket.

2. Stick your right thumb in the Green pocket and your two fingers next to it in the Yellow pocket. As you do this, raise the flaps with the names of the colors on them so that it looks like this:

3. Now you have something that looks like a paper flower. By moving your fingers and thumbs, you can open and close the Flipper in two different directions:

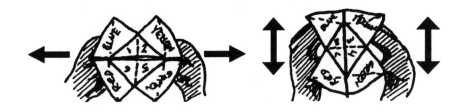

Using the Friendship Flipper With a Partner

1. Ask your partner to pick one of the four colors on the Flipper.

2. For each letter in the name of the color your partner picked, open and close the Flipper. Alternate the direction you open the Flipper with each letter. Leave the Flipper open on the last letter so that you can see the numbers.

3. Have your partner pick one of the numbers showing in the open Flipper.

4. Alternating directions, open and close the Flipper as many times as the number your partner picked. Leave the Flipper open the last time so you can see the numbers again.

5. Have your partner pick one of these numbers.

6. Open the flap in the inside of the Flipper with this number on it. Now ask your partner if they want A or B.

7. Read out loud the friendship behavior your partner has picked. Tell your partner he or she needs to do this friendship action before tomorrow!

Now its your partner's turn to use the Flipper and you pick the colors and numbers to find your own friendship behavior to do!

SUPPLEMENTARY ACTIVITY #3 HANDOUT #2

The Friendship Flipper

Directions:

Use the Friendship Flipper to decide what friendship challenge you will do today!

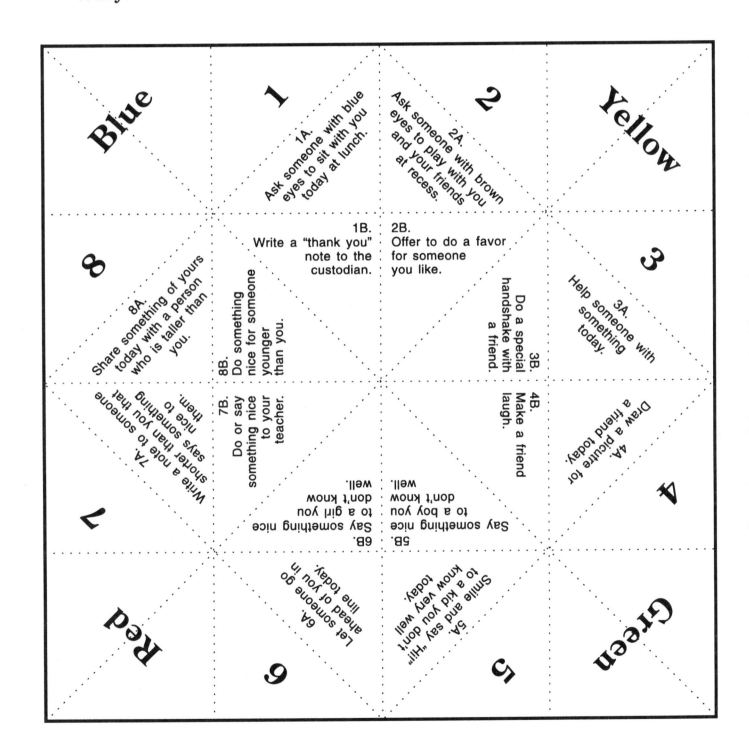

Blue

1

1A.
Ask someone with blue eyes to sit with you today at lunch.

2

2A.
Ask someone with brown eyes to play with you and your friends at recess.

Yellow

1B.
Write a "thank you" note to the custodian.

2B.
Offer to do a favor for someone you like.

8

8A.
Share something of yours today with a person who is taller than you.

3

3A.
Help someone with something today.

8B.
Do something nice for someone younger than you.

3B.
Do a special handshake with a friend.

7A.
Write a note to someone shorter than you that says something nice to them.

7B.
Do or say something nice to your teacher.

4B.
Make a friend laugh.

4A.
Draw a picture for a friend today.

6B.
Say something nice to a girl you don't know well.

5B.
Say something nice to a boy you don't know well.

4

7

6A.
Let someone go ahead of you in line today.

5A.
Smile and say "Hi!" to a kid you don't know very well today.

Red

6

Green

5

Kids' Kindness Laws

Write 5 "Kids' Kindness Laws" that would make this class a happier place for everyone.

1. _____

2. _____

3. _____

4. _____

5. _____

Write 2 things you already do to be kind.

1. _____

2. _____

Write 1 thing you might do today to be kind. Pick something you don't do a lot.

_____

How I Treat My Friends

Direcitons:

Check true ("T") or false ("F") for each of the questions below.

T	F	
☐	☐	1. I wait my turn.
☐	☐	2. I'm not bossy.
☐	☐	3. I don't cheat when I'm playing games.
☐	☐	4. I'm able to admit it when I make mistakes.
☐	☐	5. I'm able to say I'm sorry when I've hurt my friend's feelings.
☐	☐	6. I'm generous with my things.
☐	☐	7. I give compliments to my friends.
☐	☐	8. I'm honest with my friends.
☐	☐	9. I keep the secrets my friends tell me.
☐	☐	10. I do favors for my friends without expecting them to do favors in return.
☐	☐	11. I don't talk about my friends behind their backs.
☐	☐	12. I try to be fair.
☐	☐	13. I keep my promises I make to my friends.
☐	☐	14. I let my friends have other friends.
☐	☐	15. I'm able to forgive my friends when they say they are sorry about something they did to me.
☐	☐	16. I don't brag to my friends.
☐	☐	17. I listen when my friends talk instead of just thinking about what I want to say.
☐	☐	18. I take the time to help my friends learn something new.

Making a Circle of Friends

Objective

Students will identify peers they will go out of their way to be friendly to during the coming week.

Materials

Supplementary Activity #6 Handout, "A Circle of Friends," for each student

Scissors, pencil

Supplementary Activity #6 Transparency, "A Circle of Friends: Completed Cut-Out"

Procedure

Give each student a copy of the "A Circle of Friends" handout. After students do their cutting, the larger "friendly faces" will become a personal circle of friends. Use the transparency to help students visualize the steps below.

Demonstrate how to cut out the handout:

(1)

1. Cut out the square with the faces.
2. Fold the paper in half along the dotted lines. (It is important to fold as closely along the dotted lines as possible and to keep the printed side out.)

(2)

3. Fold it in half again.
4. Fold it in half one last time; turning the paper so that the figure faces you.

(3)

5. Cut away all of the black parts.
6. Unfold the "Circle of Friends."

(4)
(5)

Instruct students to write their own name on the figure labeled "ME" in the circle. Remind them that there are different kinds of friends (you may wish to use Transparency #2, "Different Kinds of Friends," from the lesson). Have them write the names of one or two of their "best friends" right beside themselves on the circle. Next, have them write the names of "playmates and regular friends" on the other figures. If they still have some figures unnamed, they may write the name of an "acquaintance" on the last figure(s). In order to help less social students save face, give everyone the option of just writing the names of people they intend to be friendly to on the remaining figures in the circle. When all figures are named, have students draw in their friends' faces and color the circle of friends.

(6)

SUPPLEMENTARY ACTIVITY #6 HANDOUT

A Circle of Friends

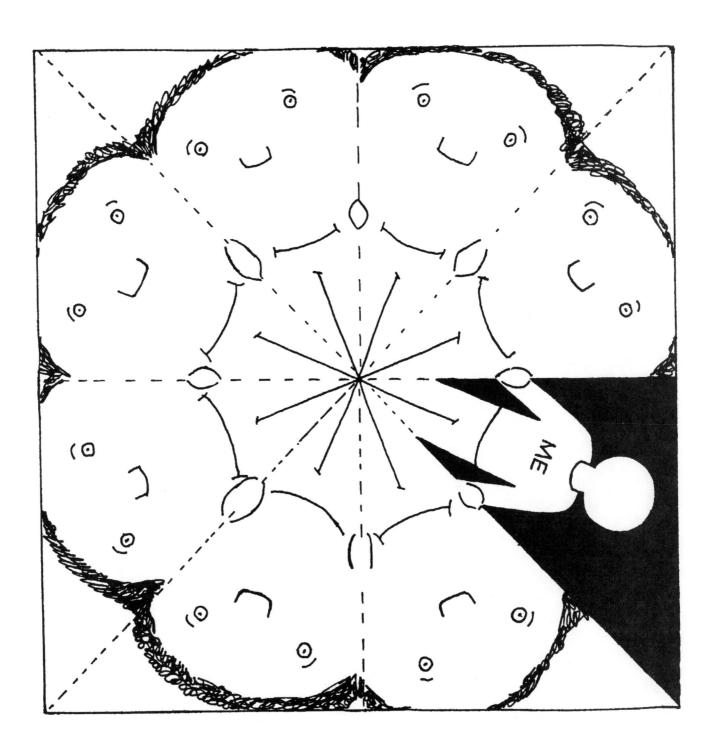

SUPPLEMENTARY ACTIVITY #6 TRANSPARENCY

A Circle of Friends: Completed Cut-Out

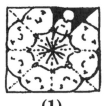 (1)    (2)   (3)   (4)(5)    (6)

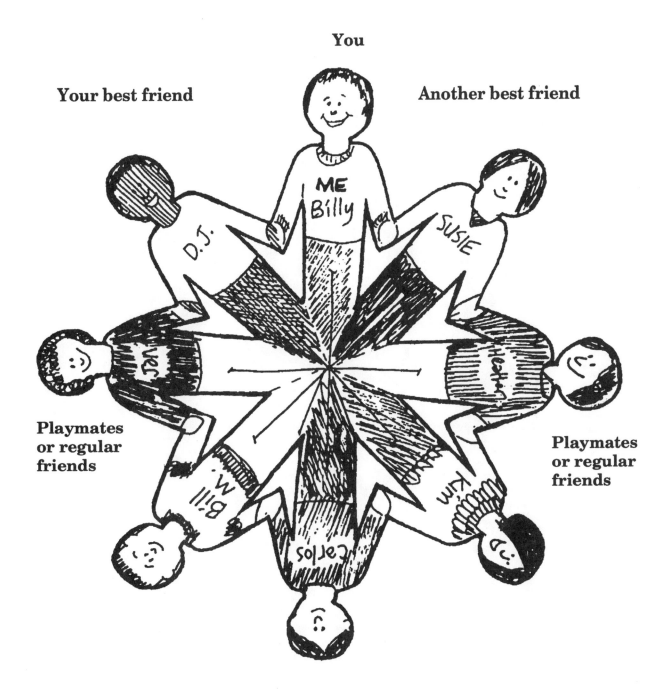

You

Your best friend

Another best friend

Playmates or regular friends

Playmates or regular friends

Acquaintances

Putting Friendship Skills Into Action

Objective

Students will practice specific behaviors that promote friendship.

Students will evaluate their own friendship behavior and devise an action plan for improvement.

Materials

Lesson 4, Transparency #4 - "20 Ways You Can Make Others Feel Special"

Handouts #1A and #1B - "Role-Play Scenarios"

Handouts #2A and #2B - "Scenarios for Illustration"

Handouts #3A and #3B - "Friendship Word Search" and "Friendship Word Search Answer Key"

Transparency #1/Handout #4 - "Rate Yourself As A Friend"

Transparency #2/Handout #5 - "My Friendship Action Plan"

Handout #6 - "How I'm Doing on My Friendship Action Plan"

Scratch paper or "think pad" to write notes on

To the Teacher

In this lesson students have an opportunity to choose between doing role-plays or short skits that illustrate friendship skills or creating drawings that illustrate ways to make another feel special. Students then evaluate themselves using a scale that asks them to rate how often they perform friendship behavior. They then devise a "Friendship Action Plan," deciding on a specific friendship behavior they will work on until the next lesson.

Before beginning this lesson, run off several copies of Handouts #1A and #1B, "Role-Play Scenarios," and of Handouts #2A and #2B, "Scenarios for Illustration." Cut the handouts into strips and put them in separate containers so students can draw slips from the containers.

If your school uses a grade-leveled approach to this curriculum, the lesson itself can be taught each year as the concepts bear repeating. Students bring a new awareness level, new abilities to process, and new examples to each lesson. Use the following Supplementary Activities at these suggested grade levels. Some first grade activities can't be used until mid-year. Students can work in pairs and help each other with the reading.

1st	"Make a Friendship Pizza"
	(Supplementary Activity #1)
	"My Friendship Story"
	(Supplementary Activity #2)
2nd	"Friendship Flipper Fortune Teller"
	(Supplementary Activity #3)
	"Make the Face Fit the Words"
	(Supplementary Activity #4)
	"Give a Little Help When You Can"
	(Supplementary Activity #5)
3rd	"Fairness Is . . ."
	(Supplementary Activity #6)
	"My Helping Diary"
	(Supplementary Activity #7)

Lesson Presentation

REVIEW OF LESSON 4

Raise your hand if you remember the secret to making friends that we talked about in our last lesson. *Allow for student response.* **Last week we talked about at least 20 ways to make a person feel special. Turn to your Learning Partner and decide who is taller. I'd like the taller person to tell your Learning Partner as many ways as you can think of to make someone feel special. I'd like the shorter person to make a mark on your "think pad" or a piece of scratch paper for each thing your partner mentions.** *Give students time to do this, then ask the shorter Learning Partner:* **Did anybody's learning partner think of 15 things? How many had a learning partner who thought of ten things? Of five things?**

Lesson 4, Transp. #4

Now I'd like the shorter Learning Partner to tell the taller partner one thing you did since our last lesson to make someone feel special. *Allow time for this, then show Lesson 4, Transparency #4, "20 Ways You Can Make Others Feel Special," and review it with students. After the review, ask if any students remembered doing something kind they hadn't thought of earlier.*

ROLE-PLAYING AND ILLUSTRATING WAYS TO MAKE OTHERS FEEL SPECIAL

Handout #1A
Handout #1B
Handout #2A
Handout #2B

Have ready the containers with handouts of role-play scenarios and scenarios for illustration (Handouts #1A, #1B, #2A, and #2B). Say: **Let's practice some more ways to make someone feel special. This time, I'm going to ask you to draw a slip of paper that describes a situation where you could choose to do something to make someone feel good and want to be your friend. You can either act out the situation with a partner or you can draw a picture showing what you would do to make the person feel special.** *Have students who wish to do role-plays find a partner. Have each pair draw two slips from the container holding the Role-Play Scenarios. Let them choose the one they like the best to role-play. They can place the other slip back in the container. Allow these students to go to different corners of the room or hall to practice their role-play quietly. Have students who prefer to illustrate a scenario draw two slips from the container holding the Scenarios for Illustration. Let them choose the one they like the best to illustrate. Have students put a title on their picture.*

After teams have had enough time for practice, have them return to their seats and ask students to stop work on their illustrations so that everyone can watch the role-plays. Assure students who have not completed their drawings that they will have time to finish after watching the role-plays.

Challenge students to try to guess which way of making someone feel special each role-play team is dramatizing. Coach role-play teams as necessary to help them appropriately demonstrate their friendship skill.

Handout #3A
Handout #3B

When all the role-plays are completed, allow the role-players to do Handout #3A, "Friendship Word Search," so they will be occupied while other students complete their illustrations. They can then check their word searches with the answer key, Handout #3B ("Friendship Word Search Answer Key"). Students who finish their illustrations quickly can also do the word search. Allow students to show their illustrations to the class or create a special bulletin board for them.

KINDNESS ENGENDERS KINDNESS

As a way of summarizing the prosocial behavior presented in the lesson, put a very large rubber band around your finger. (The type used in aerobic classes would be great.) Stretch it out and let it fall back lightly a couple of times. Say: **What goes out comes back just like this rubber band. The nice things that come out from you to others will come back to you at some time. When you're nice to others it usually makes them want to be nice to you. When you're mean to others it makes it hard for them to like you.**

SELF-EVALUATION REGARDING FRIENDSHIP BEHAVIORS

**Handout #4
Transp. #1**

Give students Handout #4, "Rate Yourself As A Friend," and show the transparency of the same title. Say or paraphrase: **Now that you know several ways to make others feel special, I'd like you to think about how often you do these behaviors. Don't look at anyone's paper but your own. This activity is private and no one will see your paper but you. You will need it to do our next activity. As I read each behavior ask yourself, "Do I always do this?" "Do I sometimes do this?" or "Do I need to work on this?" You would check the last column if you feel you should do something a little more often than you do. Be honest with yourself. This way you can see which friendship behaviors you are already good at and which behaviors you could improve.**

DECIDING ON AN "ACTION PLAN" FOR IMPROVING FRIENDSHIP BEHAVIOR

**Handout #5
Transp. #2**

Give students Handout #5, "My Friendship Action Plan," and put the transparency of the same title on the overhead. Model filling out the "Friendship Action Plan" yourself or fill it out as an imaginary student. Answer the first two questions, then formulate a goal or a specific way to make someone feel special. You might want to model this again, coming up with different responses to each question. Ask students to complete the handout using their responses on the rating sheet (Handout #4) to help them; tell them you would like to look at their action plan but not their rating sheet.

Handout #6

Promote implementation of students' action plans by having them identify specific times they're going to do the behavior they chose to work on. If you see a student enacting their action plan, reinforce them for doing so. At the end of each day for the next few days, ask students to take out Handout #6, "How I'm Doing on My Friendship Action Plan," and color in the happy or sad faces, as appropriate. Praise those students who remembered their action plan and encourage the rest to do their targeted behavior after school or during the next day.

LESSON REVIEW

Review the lesson by asking students to tell their Learning Partner the main secret to making friends. Give them the answer — "Make others feel special!" Have those students whose partners have the correct answer raise their hands. Continue the lesson review by doing a "whip" around the room, asking students to respond to one of these sentence starters:

- *I learned . . . .*

- *I was surprised that . . . .*

- *What I'll remember most is . . . .*

- *Something I'll do as a result of this lesson is . . . .*

Use the Supplementary Activities to provide additional practice with lesson skills and concepts.

Role-Play Scenarios

1. Let the Person Have Other Friends

Your best friend and you have planned on getting together on Saturday to play computer games. Your friend comes up to you and says that he or she wants to get together with another friend to see a movie that's playing at the same time you were going to get together. Your friend asks if you can get together at another time instead. Show how you could make your friend feel special by letting him or her have other friends.

2. Be a Good Sport

You really wanted to win the game you were playing with a friend, but instead of winning you really lost big! The other person is happy to have won. Show how you could make this person feel special by being a good sport about losing.

3. Let the Person Go First

Your class is having a special ice cream treat. You and your friend both get to the ice cream line at the same time. Act out how you could make your friend feel special by letting him or her go first.

4. Offer to Help Them

Your class is working on an art project. You notice that the person next to you is having a hard time putting a project together because he or she needs to hold a piece while gluing it. Show how you could make this person feel special by offering to help them.

5. Give the Person a Compliment

Someone you like did something that you thought was really neat. Show how you could make this person feel special by giving them a compliment about what they did.

Role-Play Scenarios (continued)

6. Forgive Them if They Do Something Wrong

Someone you like wasn't looking where he or she was walking in the cafeteria and bumped into you. Your tray was knocked out of your hands and some of the food spilled all over your clothes! The person was embarrassed and he or she apologized and started to clean it up. Show how you could make the person feel better by forgiving them.

7. Ask the Person to Be Your Partner

You are out on a field trip to a museum. The teacher says that everyone should sit on the bus with a partner. Instead of waiting to see if someone picks you, you decide to ask someone who you want to be friends with to sit with you. Show how you would make this person feel special by asking them to be your partner.

8. Stick Up for Someone

Someone on your team misses catching a fly ball during a baseball game. The other kids on the team are mad because you're losing the game. They start calling him or her "fumble fingers" and "klutz." You could tell that the sun was right in the person's eyes so that the ball was hard to catch. Show how you could make the person feel special by sticking up for them.

9. Apologize When You're Wrong

You laughed at your friend's haircut. You can see that you hurt his or her feelings. Show how you could make your friend feel better by apologizing.

10. Keep Someone's Secret

Someone who knows you and your friend comes up and asks you what your friend was whispering in your ear. What was whispered was a secret your friend was sharing with you. Make your friend feel special by not telling his or her secret to this other person. What will you say to the person asking you to tell?

Scenarios for Illustration

A. Offer to Let Them Borrow Something

The person next to you is trying to find a yellow crayon but not having any luck. You are through using your yellow crayon. Show how you could make this person feel special by offering to let them borrow yours.

B. Ask the Person to Play With You

You see someone on the playfield you would like to get to know better. This person isn't playing with anyone else right now. Show how you could make this person feel special by asking them to play with you.

C. Offer to Share Things

You have a small bag of cookies for a snack. You are about to eat a piece when you notice that the person next to you doesn't have a snack to eat. Show how you could make this person feel special by sharing some of your cookies with them.

D. Invite the Person Over

There is a person in your class you know pretty well and would like to be better friends with. Show how you could make this person feel special by inviting them over to your place to play.

E. Call Them on the Phone

You have a new friend who you are just getting to know. You just got a new bike! Show how you could make this person feel special by calling them up on the phone to talk to them.

Scenarios for Illustration (continued)

F. Offer to Share Things

You have a baseball mitt but your friend doesn't. Show how you could make your friend feel special by offering to share your mitt with them.

G. Offer to Help If Someone Gets Hurt

You are on your way to class. You see someone fall down and cut their knee. Show how you could make this person feel special by offering to go to the office with them so that they can get a bandage for their knee.

H. Offer to Help Someone

You see someone having trouble with a hard math problem. You know how to figure out the answer. In your class your teacher likes you to help each other with math. Show how you could make this person feel special by offering to help them.

I. Teach Someone Something You Know

You know how to play a certain game or do an activity really well and your friend has never done it before. Show how you could make your friend feel special by teaching him or her how to play the game or do the activity.

J. Keep Your Promises

You know you will be getting a bike for your birthday and you promise your friend that he or she can ride it. When your birthday comes, the bike you get is so terrific that you're not sure you want anyone else to touch it or ride it. Show how you can make your friend feel special by keeping your promise.

HANDOUT #3A

Friendship Word Search

Directions:

Find all the friendship words or short phrases listed at the bottom of the page that are hidden below.

```
K  K  G  V  A  R  G  H  T  D  R  Z  D  K  E  H
E  X  E  O  R  N  E  O  N  I  C  E  E  P  R  U
E  E  N  E  I  D  N  N  X  H  E  L  P  F  U  L
P  N  E  P  P  N  E  E  F  D  B  O  E  L  C  F
S  C  R  O  J  P  R  S  A  P  R  Y  N  I  O  C
S  O  O  Y  S  A  R  T  A  N  L  A  D  S  O  O
E  U  U  C  H  I  E  O  L  I  D  L  A  T  P  M
C  R  S  S  A  R  A  L  M  N  B  E  B  E  E  P
R  A  N  F  X  R  E  N  I  I  E  A  L  N  R  L
E  G  L  C  N  T  I  K  P  S  S  R  E  M  A  I
T  E  S  M  I  L  I  N  G  Q  I  E  Z  Y  T  M
S  I  V  H  A  P  P  O  G  A  M  O  S  N  I  E
S  T  E  U  N  I  Q  U  E  I  S  H  F  R  V  N
G  O  O  D  S  P  O  R  T  M  Y  G  U  M  E  T
V  O  F  R  N  F  O  R  G  I  V  E  N  X  S  P
```

CARING	FUN	**KIND**
COMPLIMENT	GENEROUS	LISTEN
COOPERATIVE	GOOD SPORT	LOYAL
DEPENDABLE	HELPFUL	NICE
ENCOURAGE	HONEST	**SHARE**
FAIR	**KEEP PROMISES**	SMILING
FORGIVE	KEEPS SECRETS	UNIQUE

*Clue: The words in **bold** are written diagonally.*

HANDOUT #3B—ANSWER SHEET

Friendship Word Search Answer Key

Directions:

Find all the friendship words or short phrases listed at the bottom of the page that are hidden below.

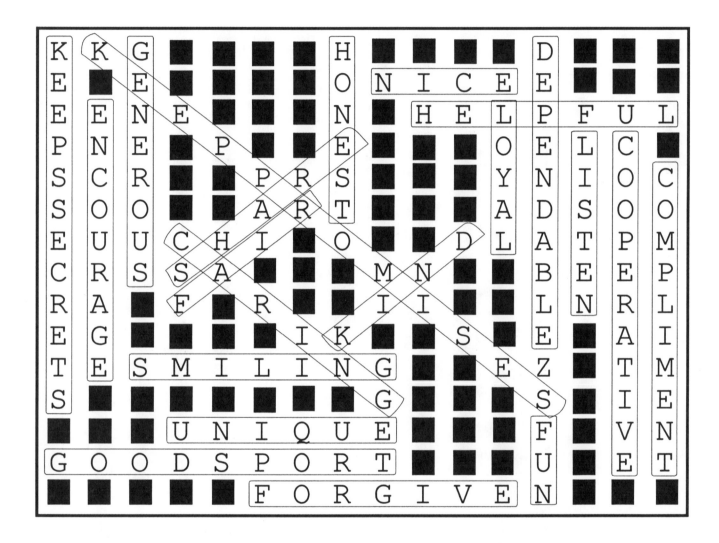

CARING	FUN	**KIND**
COMPLIMENT	GENEROUS	LISTEN
COOPERATIVE	GOOD SPORT	LOYAL
DEPENDABLE	HELPFUL	NICE
ENCOURAGE	HONEST	**SHARE**
FAIR	**KEEP PROMISES**	SMILING
FORGIVE	KEEPS SECRETS	UNIQUE

*Clue: The words in **bold** are written diagonally.*

Rate Yourself As A Friend

Directions:

For each question check the box that best describes you.

	I always do this	I sometimes do this	I need to work on this
1. I ask my friends what they would like to play.	❑	❑	❑
2. I let my friends go first.	❑	❑	❑
3. I play fair.	❑	❑	❑
4. I'm a good sport.	❑	❑	❑
5. I share things with my friends.	❑	❑	❑
6. I offer to help my friends with things.	❑	❑	❑
7. I am honest with my friends.	❑	❑	❑
8. I offer to do favors for my friends.	❑	❑	❑
9. I listen when my friends talk.	❑	❑	❑
10. I encourage my friends.	❑	❑	❑
11. I keep promises and secrets.	❑	❑	❑
12. I forgive my friends if they do something wrong.	❑	❑	❑
13. I let my friends have other friends.	❑	❑	❑
14. I give my friends compliments.	❑	❑	❑

TRANSPARENCY #2/HANDOUT #5

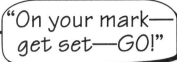

"On your mark—get set—GO!"

"Clean up your act!"

My Friendship Action Plan

1. I'm already good at . . .

A. _____

B. _____

2. I could be a little better at . . .

A. _____

B. _____

3. ONE thing I will start doing to make others feel special is . . .

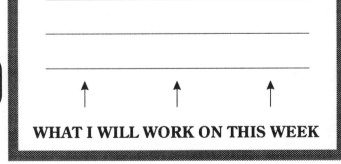

_____
_____
_____
_____
_____

↑ ↑ ↑

WHAT I WILL WORK ON THIS WEEK

"Get it together!"

"Let's see some ACTION!"

If you want a friend— be one!

HANDOUT #6

How I'm Doing on My Friendship Action Plan

Directions:

- Each time you did what you said you'd do in your action plan, color a

- If you ignored or forgot to do it, color the

- My action plan is to try to: _____

_____.

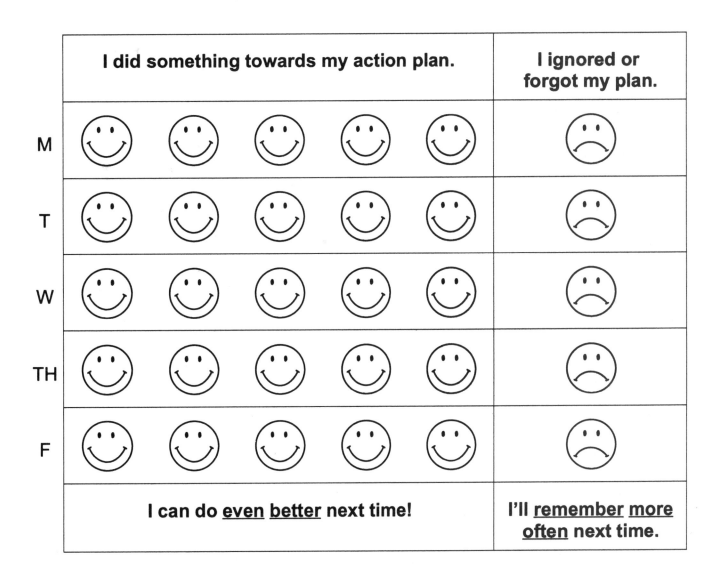

	I did something towards my action plan.					I ignored or forgot my plan.
M	☺	☺	☺	☺	☺	☹
T	☺	☺	☺	☺	☺	☹
W	☺	☺	☺	☺	☺	☹
TH	☺	☺	☺	☺	☺	☹
F	☺	☺	☺	☺	☺	☹
	I can do <u>even</u> <u>better</u> next time!					**I'll <u>remember</u> <u>more</u> <u>often</u> next time.**

Make a Friendship Pizza

Directions:

1. Cut out the toppings below that have comments that would make a person feel special, then paste these onto the pizza on the next page.

2. Cut out the toppings with the mean comments and dump these in the trash can on the other page **or** you can put them on your pizza, but only if you cross out the mean comments and write in friendly ones instead!

SUPPLEMENTARY ACTIVITY #1 HANDOUT #1

My Friendship Pizza

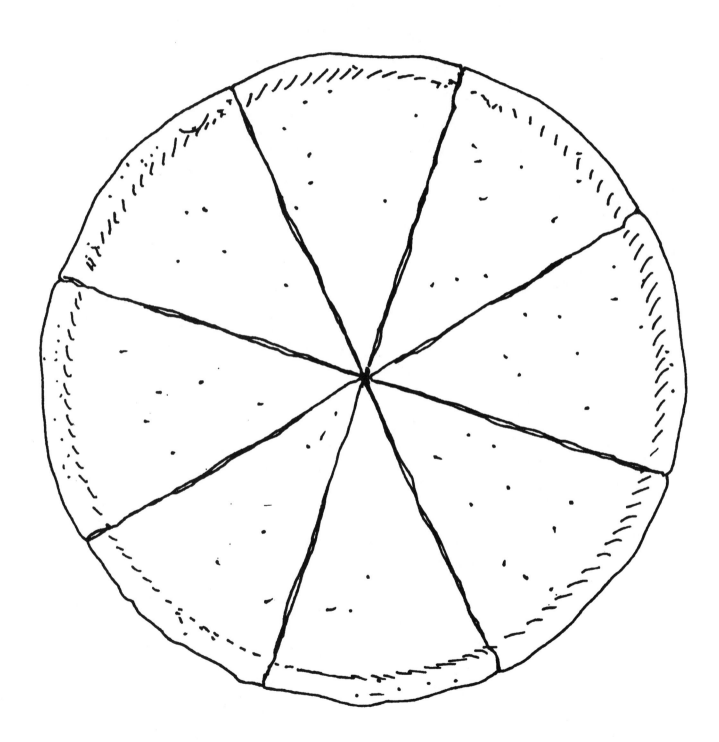

Put Mean Words Where They Belong

My Friendship Story

Objective   Students will focus on friendly behaviors by making up a story about themselves.

Materials   Picture-story paper with lines for writing and space for drawing

Crayons

Procedure   Tell students they are going to write and illustrate a story about themselves. This story is going to be about a day they decided to be friendly. They will be friendly when they get up in the morning. They will be friendly to classmates and friendly to people they play with in the neighborhood. The story can be about a day at school or some other time. Tell students they will have an opportunity to share their stories with the rest of the class.

SUPPLEMENTARY ACTIVITY #3

Friendship Flipper Fortune Teller

Directions:

- Even though there's no way to tell the future, just for fun, try using this Friendship Flipper Fortune Teller with a friend!

- Use the directions from "The Friendship Flipper" in Lesson 4 to make your flipper.

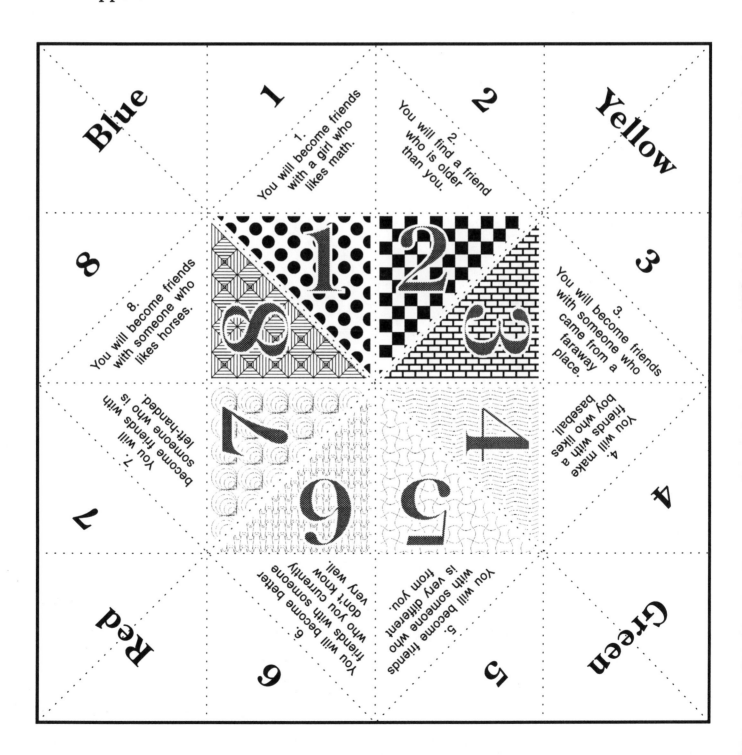

Blue

1. You will become friends with a girl who likes math.

2. You will find a friend who is older than you.

Yellow

8. You will become friends with someone who likes horses.

3. You will become friends with someone who came from a faraway place.

7. You will become friends with someone who is left-handed.

4. You will make friends with a boy who likes baseball.

Red

6. You will become better friends with someone who you currently don't know very well.

5. You will become friends with someone who is very different from you.

Green

Make the Face Fit the Words

Directions:

1. **Decide** if the statements being made by the kids on the other page would be a **friendly** or **unfriendly** thing to say.

2. **Cut out** the eyes and mouths you like below.

3. **Glue or paste** these onto the faces so that the friendly statements have friendly faces and the unfriendly statements have unfriendly faces.

4. **Draw** hair on the kids' heads.

MEAN EYES	FRIENDLY EYES

MEAN MOUTHS	FRIENDLY MOUTHS

Make the Face Fit the Words–FACES

Make the Face Fit the Words—You Make Up the Words

Directions:

Make up some mean or friendly comments and write these in the bubbles. Then make the faces fit the words.

Give a Little Help When You Can

Objective   Students will brainstorm ways to be helpful to others and illustrate the one of their choice.

Materials   Supplementary Activity #5 Handout, "Give a Little Help When You Can," for each student

Supplementary Activity #5 Transparency ("Give a Little Help When You Can")

Procedure   Engage the class in a discussion about helping behaviors by asking the following questions:

- What's a good thing to do before you help someone? (Ask if they want help.)

- Is it possible to be too helpful? Why? (Yes, there are times when others don't want help or need to learn to do something themselves.)

- What can you do when someone asks for help that you don't want to give? (Politely tell them that you aren't going to be able to help.)

Put the transparency on the overhead. Discuss the difference between the behavior of the ostrich who hides from helping others and someone who is willing to "stick their neck out" sometimes to be a good friend. Help students brainstorm ways they can be helpful in the classroom, at home, and in their neighborhoods. Write their suggestions in the box on the transparency.

Give each student a copy of the handout and instruct them to draw a picture in the box of a helping action. Tell them they can draw a way they have been helpful in the past or a way they plan to be helpful in the future, or they can illustrate one of the helping activities written on the transparency.

Don't ignore someone who needs help— stick your neck out for them!

Give a Little Help When You Can

Don't ignore someone who needs help— stick your neck out for them!

Help them find someone to play with at recess.

Help them clean up when they spill something.

Help them when their jacket zipper is stuck.

Help them find things they've lost.

Draw a picture showing how you could help someone.

Fairness Is . . .

Objective   Students will discern between fair and unfair behaviors and think of various ways to act fairly in their dealings with others.

Materials   Supplementary Activity #6 Handout, "Fairness Is . . .," for each student

Procedure   Ask students for examples of fair and unfair behavior. Give them the following examples and ask them to decide whether these show fair or unfair actions.

- Helping a friend put away a game when you've both played with it.

- Taking turns when there's only one toy.

- Giving a friend a cut in line so they don't have to go to the end.

- Letting your friend use something of yours when you've used something of his or hers.

- Taking the newest reading book every day because you're closest to the bookshelf.

- Letting your friend pick the first piece after you've cut a candy bar in half.

Give students the handout and have them check the "fair" or "unfair" box for each example. Have them finish the handout by writing their own examples of fair behavior on the lines at the bottom of the page.

Fair ☐
Unfair ☐

SUPPLEMENTARY ACTIVITY #6 HANDOUT

Fairness Is . . .

Directions:

Decide whether these actions are fair or unfair. Write in some things you think show fairness on the lines at the bottom of the page.

You helped clean up because you helped make the mess.
Fair ☐ Unfair ☐

You took the biggest piece because you are bigger.

Fair ☐ Unfair ☐

You acted like you did all the work even though other people helped, too.
Fair ☐ Unfair ☐

You went first because the other person went first last time.
Fair ☐ Unfair ☐

In baseball, you always want to pitch and won't play in the outfield.

Fair ☐ Unfair ☐

You let the other person have a turn even when you don't like the other person.
Fair ☐ Unfair ☐

Fairness is . . .

_____

_____

_____

_____

_____

My Helping Diary

Objective

Students will focus on helping others by keeping a daily journal of ways they help.

Materials

Supplementary Activity #7 Handout, "My Helping Diary: Ways I've Helped Others This Week"

Procedure

Tell students that they are going to make notes each day about ways they have been helpful to others and that at the end of the week they will have an opportunity to share. Give students a few minutes each day to reflect on their helpful behaviors and to make notations on their diary pages. Suggest that they use initials instead of names when they refer to someone in their diary.

At the end of the week, give volunteers an opportunity to tell some of the ways they were helpful; remind them not to use names or to share anything that would embarrass someone. Ask students the following types of questions:

- How did you feel about helping others?

- What were some of the hard times? The easy times?

- How did others respond to you when you were helpful?

- How did you feel about yourself when you were doing something to help someone else?

- What are some ways you can be helpful to others outside the classroom?

MONDAY
I helped Julia
with her chores.

SUPPLEMENTARY ACTIVITY #7 HANDOUT

My Helping Diary
Ways I've Helped Others This Week

MONDAY

TUESDAY

WEDNESDAY

THURSDAY

FRIDAY

How to Give a Compliment

Objective   Students will learn to give a variety of compliments to classmates using a set of three steps.

Materials   Transparency #1 - "Cold Prickly"

Transparency #2 - "Warm Fuzzy"

Transparency #3 - "Steps for Giving a Compliment"

Transparency #4 - "Every Person Is a Mix of Things You Like and Things You Don't Like"

Transparency #5 - "Three Ways to Compliment People"

Transparency #6/Handout #1 - "Compliments: Sentence Starters and Words"

Transparency #7/Handout #2 - "Fuzzy-Gram"

Transparency #8 - "Who to Give Your Warm Fuzzies and Compliments To"

Warm Fuzzy Holder

Warm Fuzzy House

Small pom-pom balls available at craft or fabric stores (Warm Fuzzies)

Small rubber balls with "spikes" from toy stores (Cold Pricklies)

Class list cut up with girls' and boys' names in separate cups

Poster - "We only give Fuzzies."

To The Teacher   "The deepest principle in human nature is the desire to be appreciated." — *William James*

Being able to give and accept compliments gracefully is a skill that can help students make and keep friends. Communicating appreciation is an excellent way to show interest in another person. The ability to give and accept a sincere compliment is a key skill for life and can help students become more comfortable in social situations.

Students who know how to engage in positive exchanges will have a much better chance of establishing good interpersonal relations with future peers, teachers, and employers. They will find that people will react to them in a more friendly and supportive manner.

The best way to teach students to be more positive is to model giving compliments to them and to provide a setting in which they can comfortably practice giving compliments to one another. Some children receive few compliments at home or at school, and appreciation from a peer can mean a great deal to these students. By setting up a "compliment nourishment distribution system" in your classroom, some students will get the acknowledgment and affirmation they crave, and as a result can bring more attention to their academic tasks.

Often children feel embarrassed about giving a compliment. Some fear rejection and hold back from complimenting. Others have simply never learned how to give compliments. In this lesson students will practice the steps of giving a compliment so that this becomes a natural part of their social interaction.

A good way to introduce the skill of giving compliments is to tape to each student's desk a "Warm Fuzzy Holder" or "Warm Fuzzy House" containing eight or ten Warm Fuzzies. (Small pom-pom balls work well as Warm Fuzzies; these are available in many different colors in craft or fabric stores, often with 100 to a package.) The holder or house should also be stocked with several "Fuzzy-Grams" (Handout #2).

Before the contents of the holder are explained to students, tell them "The Warm Fuzzy Story" in this lesson. As you tell the story, you might want to toss out a few Cold Pricklies and Warm Fuzzies at appropriate times. (For Cold Pricklies you can use the small rubber balls with spikes on them which are available in most toy stores.) After the story, explain that students will be giving their Warm Fuzzies away, but ask them not to touch the contents of their Warm Fuzzy Holders until you tell them to do so.

The Warm Fuzzy Story that follows was inspired by: *Fuzzies*, written by Richard Lessor; *Swabedoo-dahs*, author unknown; and *The Original Warm Fuzzy Tale* by Claude H. Steiner.

If your school uses a grade-leveled approach to this curriculum, the lesson itself can be taught again each year. The concepts bear repeating, and students bring a new awareness level, new abilities to process, and new examples each time around. Use the following Supplementary Activities at these suggested grade levels:

1st   "The Warm Fuzzy Compliment Chair"
           (Supplementary Activity #1)
      "You Are a Star in Many Ways"
           (Supplementary Activity #2)
      "A Warm Fuzzy Reinforcement System"
           (Supplementary Activity #3)

2nd   "Making and Giving Warm Fuzzies"
            (Supplementary Activity #4)
        "Send a Critter With a Compliment"
            (Supplementary Activity #5)
        "Who Do You Think of When You Hear the Word . . . ."
            (Supplementary Activity #6)

3rd   "The Mystery Star"
            (Supplementary Activity #7)
        "Keeping Track of Compliments"
            (Supplementary Activity #8)
        "Warm Fuzzy Notes"
            (Supplementary Activity #9)
        "Walk the Line With Compliments or Put-Downs"
            (Supplementary Activity #10)

Lesson Presentation

THE WARM FUZZY STORY

Say to the students: **You have learned that the secret of friendship is to make others feel special. Today we're going to look at a great way to make others feel special. You'll be using the Warm Fuzzies in the Warm Fuzzy Holder on your desk at the end of the lesson. I'd like to start by telling you a story. Everyone get comfortable and I'll read it to you. You can put your head down on your desk or lean back in your chair. Just relax, like you were a heavy bag of sand in your chair.**

> Once upon a time in a faraway land there was a little village high on a hill. The people who lived in this village were strange, cold people. The Cold People lived in little gray houses that were cold and dark inside, and all they ate was a cold, thin porridge once a day. They wore dark, ugly clothing and walked with their shoulders hunched over. They never smiled and hardly ever spoke, and they each carried a black bag made of rough and scratchy material slung over their drooping shoulders.
>
> Every morning after the Cold People got out of their hard beds and ate their cold, thin porridge, they would sling their black bags over their shoulders and trudge out onto the frozen street.
>
> (continued)

Whenever two of the Cold People happened to meet, they would each stop, reach into their scratchy bags and take out a cold, hard ball covered with prickles. They would give each other this cold, prickly ball, and then be on their dreary way. Sometimes they wouldn't even look at each other. Other times they would say something like, "Your hair looks terrible; why don't you shave it off?" or "Well, you're certainly looking uglier than ever today!" or just "Drop dead." Giving Cold Pricklies like this was the way it was in the chilly, dark village, and this was the way it had always been.

Then one cold, blustery night a baby was born in a small dark shack on the edge of the village—it was a strange-looking baby for a Cold Person. Instead of being all wrinkly, fussy, and whining, it had warm, smooth skin, bright eyes, wisps of shining hair on its head, and it seemed to almost always be smiling.

The mother thought such a strange baby needed a strange name, and so she named it Zephyr, which means "warm breeze." She wrapped baby Zephyr in a dark shawl and fed it cold porridge, as the Cold People always did, but the baby didn't grow the way Cold babies were supposed to grow. It grew rosy and chubby and it made strange, cheerful gurgling sounds.

The Cold People came from miles around to see this strange new baby and to bring it Cold Pricklies, which were the only things they could think of to give. As they each filed by with gloomy looks on their faces, they reached into their scratchy bags and pulled out a Cold Prickly and gave it to baby Zephyr. "What an ugly baby," some of them said. "It's so weird looking. I'll bet it grows up to be stupid," said others. Most of them just handed out a Cold Prickly, and sort of pretended the baby wasn't really there, because they didn't know how to be nice.

Zephyr's mother was worried about the baby being so different. She put little Zephyr in a dark, drafty corner of the room and surrounded her baby with the Cold Pricklies from the villagers. She thought that maybe they would help Zephyr become the way babies were supposed to be in their village.

(continued)

When Zephyr's mother went outdoors to gather icicles for their thin porridge, the baby picked up each gift with a baby smile on its face. Even though the Pricklies were cold and hard, little Zephyr snuggled each one in soft baby arms and made happy sounds that were almost like singing.

Day after day little Zephyr sat in the dark corner, rocking and singing to the small pile of Cold Pricklies. And a strange thing began to happen. It happened slowly—SO slowly that even the worried mother didn't notice. At first it was only the <u>pricklies</u>. The prickles on the Cold Pricklies began to soften—just a little. And then they softened more—and more—until they were just as fluffy and soft as the hair on little Zephyr's head! Next, those Pricklies began to warm up. All the fuzzy fluff began to get so cozy and warm you would have thought you were holding a warm kitten! Finally there was just no doubt about it—little Zephyr's Cold Pricklies had all turned into Warm Fuzzies!

One particularly dreary day Zephyr's mother came in from gathering icicles and told little Zephyr they were going to town. Little Zephyr, who had learned to walk and talk by now, gathered up all the Warm Fuzzies and tucked them into a bag that was as soft and velvety as a baby duck. Soon they were off.

As Mother trudged along the road, little Zephyr skipped beside her with the velvet-soft bag over one small shoulder. From time to time they would meet one of the Cold People from the village. Each time they did, little Zephyr would plunge a soft little hand into the velvet bag and pull out a Warm Fuzzy. With a big smile, Zephyr would push the Warm Fuzzy into the hands of the villager and say something nice to that person. The bewildered villager would quickly shove the strange warm, fuzzy thing into his or her bag and give Zephyr a Cold Prickly in return.

By the end of the day, Zephyr's soft velvety bag was full of nothing but Cold Pricklies, and all the Warm Fuzzies had gone home with the villagers. But this didn't bother Zephyr. Zephyr knew that soon these new Cold Pricklies could also become Warm Fuzzies!

(continued)

This went on week after week, every time Zephyr went into town. Soon there were more and more Warm Fuzzies in the village. Soon there were fewer and fewer Cold Pricklies. The Cold People got confused and sometimes they would give each other a Warm Fuzzy instead of a Cold Prickly. Now and then a villager was seen with a tiny bit of a smile on his or her face, and once a happy chuckle was heard from behind a tree!

All the Cold People <u>really</u> knew something had changed the day the mayor of the village actually said something nice to some of the other villagers and deliberately handed them Warm Fuzzies! Soon many of the villagers were giving each other compliments when they handed each other a Warm Fuzzy, just like Zephyr always did. They said kind things like, "It's nice to see you," and "I like your new shirt," and "Hey, you did a really good job on that!"

As years went by the villagers became kinder and kinder to each other. They always gave each other a Warm Fuzzy and a compliment whenever they met. One day, they decided it didn't make any sense to call themselves the Cold People anymore. They were now people who had fun together and liked giving each other compliments.

Because they were so happy about their decision to change their name, the villagers decided to have a big celebration. The mayor wrote a special compliment for every person in town. Bands played as all the villagers voted that from that day forward they would be known as—can you guess what they called themselves? That's right—the Warm People! And there, right in the middle of that crowd of happy people giving out lots and lots of Warm Fuzzies and compliments, a young teenager named Zephyr smiled.

Use the following questions to discuss the story:

Would you have liked to live in the Cold Village like it was at the beginning of the story? *Allow for student response.*

Would you have liked to live in the village after it became the Warm Village? Why? Why did the little village become a much happier place to live in? *Allow for student response.* **Put your thumbs up if you'd like to try to make our classroom a friendlier place.**

Transp. #1

Put Transparency #1, "Cold Prickly," on the overhead. **Although our school isn't like the Cold Village, once in a while people give Cold Pricklies, don't they? Put your thumbs down if you've ever received a Cold Prickly at school.** *Pause.* **Let's try to at least get rid of the Cold Pricklies and meanness in our class. Let's put a big X across this Cold Prickly.** *Draw a big X across the transparency.*

Transp. #2

If Zephyr was in our class, what do you think Zephyr would do to stop the Cold Pricklies? How could we start to change our room so it would be like the Warm Village? *Display Transparency #2, "Warm Fuzzy," and write down student suggestions around the figure.* **Put your thumbs up if you'd like to try and make our classroom a friendlier place.**

COMPLIMENTS MAKE OTHERS FEEL SPECIAL

Today we're going to learn to do what Zephyr did so well—to give Warm Fuzzies. When we say giving Warm Fuzzies, we really mean giving compliments, because the two go together. Today we're going to learn how to make others feel good by giving them sincere compliments. Giving Warm Fuzzies or compliments is one of the best ways to make and keep friends. It's also a great way to make someone feel special. Listen to this example and you'll see what I mean:

> How would you feel if you worked an hour and a half on your math homework, and the kid next to you said, "I got more right than you did!" Then the kid behind you said, "Wow! You got the story problem right! You must have really studied!"

Which comment would make you feel special? *Allow for student response.*

THREE STEPS FOR GIVING A COMPLIMENT

Transp. #3

Put Transparency #3, "Steps for Giving a Compliment," on the overhead, but <u>begin by covering the three steps</u>. **When we compliment someone, there are three steps we will want to follow. The first one is easy.** *Uncover step #1.* **First you will notice something positive or good about the person—something they can do well or something you like about them. After you have noticed something you like about the person or something they are good at** *(uncover step #2),* **you will want to look at the person. If you're going to compliment someone, you want them to know you're talking to them. And then** *(uncover step #3),* **say the compliment to the person so they will know you mean it.**

Use the Marti Mouse and Jesse Jackrabbit puppets (or puppets of your own) to model the three steps by having one of the puppets give the other a sincere compliment. Tell students to watch to see if you are following the three steps listed on the transparency. **Marti has learned to do wheelies on his bike. Jesse says, "Wow! You're sure getting good at that!" Did Jesse look at Marti? Did Jesse sound sincere?**

MODELING GIVING COMPLIMENTS USING PUPPETS

Use the following scenarios to continue modeling compliments with the puppets:

- **Let's say Jesse got a new haircut. Marti says, "Jesse, you look good with your hair cut that way."**

- **Let's say Marti lost when they were playing a game, but he didn't pout or get into a bad mood. Jesse says, "You sure are a good sport, Marti."**

- **Let's say Jesse helped Marti make a cover for a social studies report. Marti says, "You've got good ideas, Jesse, and it was nice of you to help me."**

STUDENTS PRACTICE GIVING COMPLIMENTS TO PUPPETS

Tell students that they can have a turn to practice giving Jesse and Marti compliments. Read the following scenarios as you walk around the room, calling on student volunteers to deliver a compliment to one of the puppets. Remind them to use the three steps. To get a variety of compliments, call on more than one volunteer to respond to each scenario.

- **Marti made a goal in soccer and helped his team win the game.**

- **Jesse is wearing a T-shirt she decorated herself with marking pens, glitter, buttons, and ribbon.**

- **Jesse hadn't cleaned her room in two weeks and couldn't go out to play until it was done. Marti gave up an hour of free time to help Jesse clean her room.**

- **Jesse got into the championships in jump-roping at the neighborhood YMCA. She could do a cartwheel through a double-dutch rope.**

PREPARING STUDENTS TO COMPLIMENT ONE ANOTHER

You're getting really good at thinking up compliments. I think it's time for us to begin giving each other Warm Fuzzies. In a few minutes I'm going to ask you to write a compliment to someone in this class. You're going to draw a name, and that's the person you're going to write your compliment to. Some of you will have a chance to say your compliment to the person and give him or her one of your Fuzzies. The rest of you will just deliver your compliment and Fuzzy to your person's desk and they will read it to him or herself.

Transp. #4

What if you draw the name of someone you don't know very well or someone you don't like? Guess what? It's still possible to write them a sincere compliment! *Show Transparency #4, "Every Person Is a Mix of Things You Like and Things You Don't Like."*

EVERY PERSON HAS SOMETHING GOOD ABOUT THEM

Every person is a mix of things that are good and things that need improving or that aren't so neat. You might think that some people are just perfect and that others are total creeps. That's because you notice only the good things about some people, and only the bad things about others. If it's a person you like, you tend to focus just on what's neat about them. You just look at their pluses. *Point to the pluses on the person on the transparency.* **If it's a person you don't like, you only look at or think about the things that aren't so neat about them, or their minuses. You usually don't even notice that they have good things, too.** *Point to the minuses on the person on the transparency.*

Transp. #5

In our class, we're going to learn to notice the pluses, or good things, that everyone has. You don't have to like somebody to notice their pluses. You don't have to know them really well to give them a compliment. Everybody has something good about them, and there are lots of different kinds of compliments you can give. *Put Transparency #5, "Three Ways to Compliment People," on the overhead; cover the bottom two-thirds.*

THREE DIFFERENT KINDS OF COMPLIMENTS

The first kind of compliment you can give is a compliment about how a person acts. *Read the suggested compliments on the transparency and ask students to suggest others in this category. Present the next two categories of compliments on the transparency in the same manner.*

I'm going to read some compliments to you and I want you to listen and decide which type they are. If they are compliments about how a person acts, shout "Acts!" If they are about things a person does well, shout, "Does Well!" If they are about how a person looks, shout, "Looks!" *Read each of the following compliments and have students identify the type of compliment.*

- **It was nice of you to help Milo during math.** *(Acts)*

- **Hey, that's a neat jacket!** *(Looks)*

- **That sure was a good kick you made at recess.** *(Does Well)*

- **I like how you're always kidding around—you're fun to be with!** *(Acts)*

- **I thought the story you wrote was great.** *(Does Well)*

- **I like the way you're nice to everyone and that you don't put people down.** *(Acts)*

STUDENT VOLUNTEERS GIVE COMPLIMENTS TO CLASSMATES

Is there anyone who would like to give someone in our class a compliment about the way they act, something they do well, or about how they look? *Call on volunteers. If you have a large Warm Fuzzy ball, Kushball™, or beanbag, let the volunteer throw this to the person they wish to compliment. Make sure students look at the person as they give their compliment. Ask students receiving the compliment to look at the giver and say "Thank you" in an audible voice. Ask these students to also let the compliment make them feel good. After each compliment, retrieve the ball and give it to the next volunteer.*

WRITING COMPLIMENT FUZZY-GRAMS TO ONE ANOTHER

**Transp. #6
Handout #1**

Show students Transparency #6, "Compliments: Sentence Starters and Words." Give them a copy of this (Handout #1). **To make giving a compliment easy for you, I'm going to give you these examples of ways to start a compliment.** *Read through the sentence starters.* **At the bottom of the page is a list of compliment words. These will give you lots of different ways to describe how a person acts.** *Go over the compliment words, making sure that students can read them all.*

**Transp. #7
Handout #2**

Show students Transparency #7, "Fuzzy-Gram." **You each have some copies of these Fuzzy-Grams in your Warm Fuzzy Holder** *(or supply these now, Handout #2, if you chose not to use the holders)***. Use these when you write your compliment to the person whose name you'll draw. Be sure to write the person's name where it says "Dear" and sign your name where it says "From."** *Point these places out on the transparency as you model writing one or two imaginary Fuzzy-Grams.*

Now walk around the room, letting students draw classmates' names from a container (you may want to put girls' names in one container, boys' names in a second, and let students draw a name of the same gender). Tell students not to make any sounds when they draw their name, and to keep this name a secret until it's time to deliver the Fuzzy-Grams. Make sure absent students' names are pulled before those present draw names; if this is not done, there will be names left over and some students who are present won't get a Fuzzy-Gram.

Those students who complete their Fuzzy-Gram before others are done can color them or can write more Fuzzy-Grams for other classmates. When students have finished their Fuzzy-Grams, ask a few students to walk over to the desk of the student whose name they drew, read that person the Fuzzy-Gram they wrote, and then give the person their favorite color Warm Fuzzy. After a few volunteers have done this, have the rest of the class quietly get up and lay their Fuzzy-Gram and Warm Fuzzy on the desk of the person whose name they drew. If you like, ask for some students to volunteer to read the Fuzzy-Gram they received.

Have students keep "Compliments: Sentence Starters and Words" (Handout #1) in their folders for future reference, or collect these handouts and have students refer to a poster you've made of these words.

Say or paraphrase: **In the days ahead you can give lots more Fuzzy-Grams and Warm Fuzzies to each other. Remember, the two always go together.** *(If you are not using the Warm Fuzzy Holders, you will need to rephrase the next few lines. Otherwise, say:)* **You can put these in each others' Warm Fuzzy Holders.**

I'd like to point out what it says on your Warm Fuzzy Holders: "Fuzzies are meant to be given."; "End your day by giving your Fuzzies away!"; "Don't let your Fuzzies stay for long!"; "Keep those Fuzzies Moving!"; "Make someone's day—give a Fuzzy away!"; and "What counts is how many Fuzzies you give, not how many Fuzzies you get!"

If you want to help us try to make our classroom like Warm Village in the story, then you shouldn't try to collect Fuzzies for yourself. Instead, you should try to think of people to give Fuzzies and compliments to.

Transp. #8

Show Transparency #8, "Who to Give Your Warm Fuzzies and Compliments To." Read through the transparency. Read it once again, leaving out the last word or two on each line, and have students shout out the missing words. Ask them to picture in their minds who they are going to give their next Fuzzy-Gram to. Then ask them to picture two more people they are going to compliment, using two of the suggestions on the transparency.

LESSON REVIEW

So, today you learned the three steps for giving a compliment. You learned that everyone has something good that you can compliment them about, and that there are three types of compliments that you can give. You also learned who to give Fuzzies and compliments to. I'd like you to remember that these things you'll be doing are what the Cold People learned to do in the story, and that by doing them our classroom will be a warm and friendly place for everyone.

Have students complete the following sentence stems:

- *Now I understand better how to . . . .*
- *The way I'm going to use what I learned today is . . . .*
- *I wish . . . .*

Posters

To remind students of the concepts presented in this lesson, hang up posters of Transparencies #5, #6, and #8, plus the poster "We only give Fuzzies." found at the end of the lesson.

Most students will need a great deal of practice in order to develop a habit of noticing the positive attributes of others and giving true and sincere compliments. Supplementary Activities are included to provide this practice in giving compliments.

Cold Prickly

TRANSPARENCY #2

Warm Fuzzy

Steps for Giving a Compliment

1. Notice something you like about the person or something they are good at.

2. Look at the person.

3. Say the compliment in a way that sounds like you mean it.

Every Person Is a Mix of Things You Like and Things You Don't Like

Three Ways to Compliment People

Compliments: Sentence Starters and Words

Compliment Sentence Starters

- "I think you are . . . ."
- "You are really . . . ."
- "I like the way you are so . . . ."

Compliment Words

artistic	funny	honest
clever	generous	kind
creative	good at . . .	neat
fair	good athlete	nice
friendly	good sport	smart
fun	great	strong
	helpful	

TRANSPARENCY #7/HANDOUT #2

Fuzzy-Gram

FUZZY-GRAM

Dear ____________________,

____

____

From, ____________________

FUZZY-GRAM

Dear ____________________,

____

____

From, ____________________

FUZZY-GRAM

Dear ____________________,

____

____

From, ____________________

Who to Give Your Warm Fuzzies and Compliments To

Give one to . . .

- Someone you like a lot.

- Someone you'd like to know better.

- Someone who has done something well.

- Someone you don't usually play with.

- Someone who needs cheering up.

Warm Fuzzy Holder

End your day by giving your Fuzzies away!

Fuzzies are meant to be given.

Make someone's day—give a Fuzzy away!

Don't let your Fuzzies stay for long!

What counts is how many Fuzzies you give, not how many Fuzzies you get!

"Keep those Fuzzies moving!"

Directions:

1.
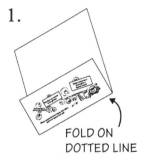
FOLD ON DOTTED LINE

2.

STAPLE

3.
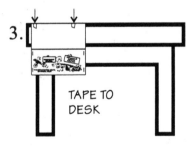
TAPE TO DESK

Warm Fuzzy House

Directions:

You can store your Warm Fuzzies in this cozy little house! Cut on the thick lines, fold on the dotted lines, and paste it all together using the tabs. Your house will then be ready to tape to your desk.

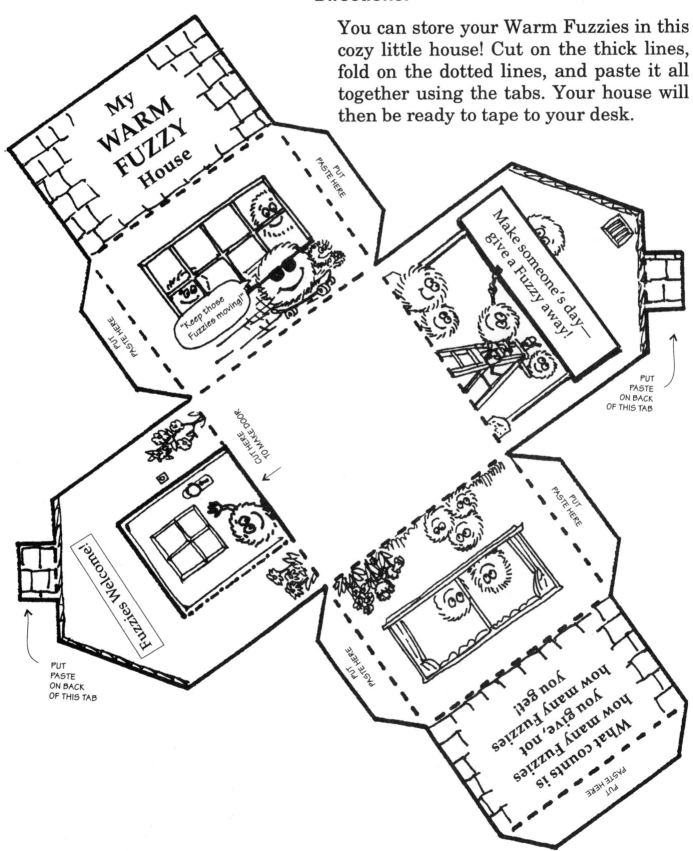

The Warm Fuzzy Compliment Chair

Objective   Students will understand that others appreciate their unique qualities.

Materials   Special chair or pillow

Procedure   Select four or five names in a random drawing of student names. Ask the students whose names were drawn to sit one at a time on the Warm Fuzzy chair or pillow. Ask the rest of the students to think about the student on the chair/pillow and try to identify things that they like about the person. When they have thought of a good quality about the person, have them raise their hand and share it. Encourage students to begin their statement with either "I like you because . . ." or "You are special because . . . ." If you limit the number of compliments or Warm Fuzzies each student gets to three or four, the time needed each time you do this activity will not be unrealistic. Wait until each student has received a stated number of compliments before going on to the next person. If you wait for a long enough period, students will come through with enough Fuzzies for everyone. Plan to participate yourself, but make sure you don't contribute compliments just for those students who you fear will receive none.

After several students have had an opportunity to receive compliments, ask these questions: How did it feel to hear your classmates saying nice things about you? Was it hard to just sit there and hear nice things about yourself? Were you surprised by some of the things you heard?

VARIATION

Ask students at some point during the day to turn to their right and give that person a compliment or Warm Fuzzy. This can be done one at a time and with four or five students per day.

You Are a Star in Many Ways

Dear _____,

The stars I have colored are the things I like about you!

From, _____

You Are:

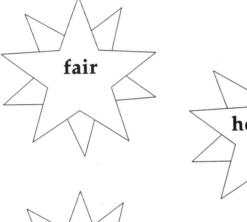

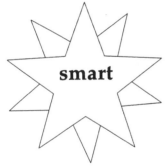

A Warm Fuzzy Reinforcement System

Objective   Students will engage in appropriate classroom behavior.

Materials   "Warm Fuzzy Behavior Chart" (Supplementary Activity #3 Handout) for each student
Small Warm Fuzzy balls

Procedure   Explain to students that you are going to tape to their desk a Warm Fuzzy chart each week and that the goal for them is to keep all six of their Warm Fuzzies each day. Explain that when they engage in inappropriate classroom behavior, they will have to place a large X through one of the Fuzzies on their chart and will not be able to color that Fuzzy at the end of the day. Establish with students the number of Fuzzies they need to keep each day or each week for them to earn rewards appropriate to your class.

You may wish to keep a container filled with Warm Fuzzies on your desk. During the day, if you wish to reinforce a positive behavior you observe a student doing, you can take the Warm Fuzzy and set it on the student's desk, telling that student what it is you appreciated. At the end of the day, the Warm Fuzzies should be collected. (You may wish to put a small check by that student's name on your class list just to make sure that all students get a Warm Fuzzy now and then.)

SUPPLEMENTARY ACTIVITY #3 HANDOUT

Warm Fuzzy Behavior Chart

Making and Giving Warm Fuzzies

Objective   Students will understand the concept of a "Warm Fuzzy" and give them to one another.

Materials   "The Warm Fuzzy Story"

Decorative fringe or fuzzy balls from a craft store (or cotton balls, yarn, or fuzzy carpeting)

"Warm Fuzzy Strips" (Supplementary Activity #4 Handout)

Procedure   Read "The Warm Fuzzy Story" to students and then discuss the meaning of a "Warm Fuzzy." Explain that Warm Fuzzies are like compliments. They're soft little creatures that we give to others when: (1) we want them to feel good, (2) when we want to show that we like them, (3) when we want to show that we appreciate something, and (4) when we think someone may need cheering up for one reason or another.

Discuss with students the meaning of a "Cold Prickly." Explain that a "Cold Prickly" is like a put-down. It is something we do or say to someone that doesn't make them feel good.

You may wish to ask for volunteers to act out or role-play some examples of Warm Fuzzies and Cold Pricklies.

Discuss these questions with students:

- How do Warm Fuzzies make you feel?
- When do you give Warm Fuzzies?
- How would you teach someone about Warm Fuzzies if that person didn't seem to know about them?
- Why is it important to give Warm Fuzzies?
- Are more Warm Fuzzies or Cold Pricklies given in your class?

Discuss with students how they can develop a system of Warm Fuzzy exchange within the class. For example, whenever a student does a favor for another student, a Warm Fuzzy can be given to him or her. When students have a special feeling of liking someone, they can give that person a Warm Fuzzy. When students see someone who looks discouraged, they can give a Warm Fuzzy.

Students can select from the following ways to make their own Warm Fuzzies:

- Use decorative fringe found in craft or sewing supply stores by simply cutting the balls off the fringe and gluing tiny craft shop eyes on them. Students can easily make a large quantity of Fuzzies. Cotton balls can also be used.

- Cut yarn into 1-1/2" strips, tie one of the lengths around the middle of the rest, and then fluff.

- A flat Fuzzy can be made by cutting furry carpeting into little circles or strips and attaching eyes.

- Cut circles out of construction paper and draw Fuzzies on them.

- Cut up the strips of Fuzzies using the Supplementary Activity #4 Handout, "Warm Fuzzy Strips."

SUPPLEMENTARY ACTIVITY #4 HANDOUT

Warm Fuzzy Strips

SUPPLEMENTARY ACTIVITY #5

Send a Critter With a Compliment

Directions:

Color the little critter below that you like the best. **Think of someone** you like, someone you want to make feel good, or someone who needs cheering up. **Write in a compliment** for that person in the box or book the critter is carrying. **Cut out** the completed card, and **give it** to the person you picked.

Who Do You Think of When You Hear the Word . . .

Objective   Students will name classmates who they think demonstrate specific positive qualities.

Materials   Supplementary Activity #6 Transparency, "Compliment Words"

Procedure   Cover the words on the transparency. Uncover each word, one at a time, and read it. Then ask questions such as the following:

- Who can think of a person in our class who is **caring**?

- Who in our class is nearly always **cheerful**?

- Who do you think of when you hear the word **fair**?

- Who in here is very **dependable**—when they say they'll do something, they do it?

- Who do you think is a very **forgiving** person in this room—someone who doesn't hold a grudge?

- Who in here is a **good listener**? Think of someone who doesn't interrupt you when you're talking to them, and who is interested in what you say.

Call on students who raise their hands and ask them to look at the person they think has the quality you've just named. Have the student say that person's name out loud for all to hear.

As you go through the list, ask students to listen carefully so they can try to name classmates who haven't been mentioned yet.

Compliment Words

caring	helpful
cheerful	honest
clever	imaginative
cooperative	kind
dependable	neat
easy-going	outdoorsy
fair	patient
forgiving	polite
fun	shares
funny	talented
generous	thoughtful
good listener	understanding
good sport	unique

SUPPLEMENTARY ACTIVITY #7

The Mystery Star

Objective   The student will learn to look for the positive in others by guessing the identity of a classmate from a list of complimentary attributes.

Materials   Chart tablet

Markers

Procedure   Select one student to be the "Mystery Star" for the week. On a sheet of chart tablet, write positive attributes of this student in compliment form—a new compliment at the beginning of each day. On Friday allow the class to guess who the Mystery Star of the week is. When the Star's identity has been revealed, write his or her name at the top of the sheet and post it during the following week; begin a new sheet for the next Star. Give sheets to Stars to take home after posting.

Examples of compliments you may write are as follows:

"Have you figured out who the Mystery Star is yet?"

- You get along with your classmates and are willing to take turns.
- You have a good sense of humor and like to make jokes.
- You try hard, even on difficult assignments.
- You are always willing to help your teacher and your classmates.
- You are almost never absent.

VARIATION

You may wish to choose a different child each day to contribute the compliment. They would be "sworn to secrecy" as to the identity of the "Star." (This technique would be especially helpful in encouraging popular students to look for positive attributes in those who are less popular.)

SUPPLEMENTARY ACTIVITY #8

Keeping Track of Compliments

Directions:

Write about three times when you gave a compliment.

Who you said the compliment to	What you said	Did it make the person feel good?
1.		❏ Yes ❏ No ❏ Couldn't tell
2.		❏ Yes ❏ No ❏ Couldn't tell
3.		❏ Yes ❏ No ❏ Couldn't tell

"You sure know how to help a guy out when he needs it!"

"You're doing great!"

Warm Fuzzy Notes

Objective   The students will learn to give positive feedback in the form of compliments by writing compliment notes to their classmates.

Materials   Supplementary Activity #9 Handout, "Warm Fuzzy Notes," for each student

Scissors, crayons, colored pens, pencil

Glue, tape, or staples

12" x 18" sheet of construction paper for each student

Compliment Words list (Handout #1, "Compliments: Sentence Starters and Words")

Procedure   Tell students they will be writing "Warm Fuzzy Notes" to their class-mates and making a Warm Fuzzy "mailbox" to hang from the front of their desks so that classmates can drop Warm Fuzzy Notes into it.

Give students a piece of construction paper. Have them fold up the bottom third and staple it at the sides to make an "envelope," as illustrated. They can decorate it, then write their names on it. The top half of the construction paper can be left as it is. Help students fasten this envelope to the front of their desks so it can be used as a mailbox.

Distribute a sheet of Warm Fuzzy Notes to each student. These notes are to be filled out and delivered to each others' mailboxes. (In order to make sure that less popular students also receive notes, suggest from time to time that students write notes to at least one classmate they don't know very well or to someone they have never complimented.) You may wish to provide a stack of note-pages for more prolific note-writers. Students can refer to their Compliment Words list to give them ideas for compliments.

This activity will gather more momentum if a specific time is provided each day for writing or reading notes.

VARIATIONS

- Students can attach a hand-made Fuzzy to the Fuzzy Note if they like.

- Another way to give Warm Fuzzies is to have a "Fuzzy Box" where students place positive notes about their fellow classmates. You might like to read these aloud at the end of the day so that students get the added enjoyment of receiving a compliment in front of their peers.

Warm Fuzzy Notes

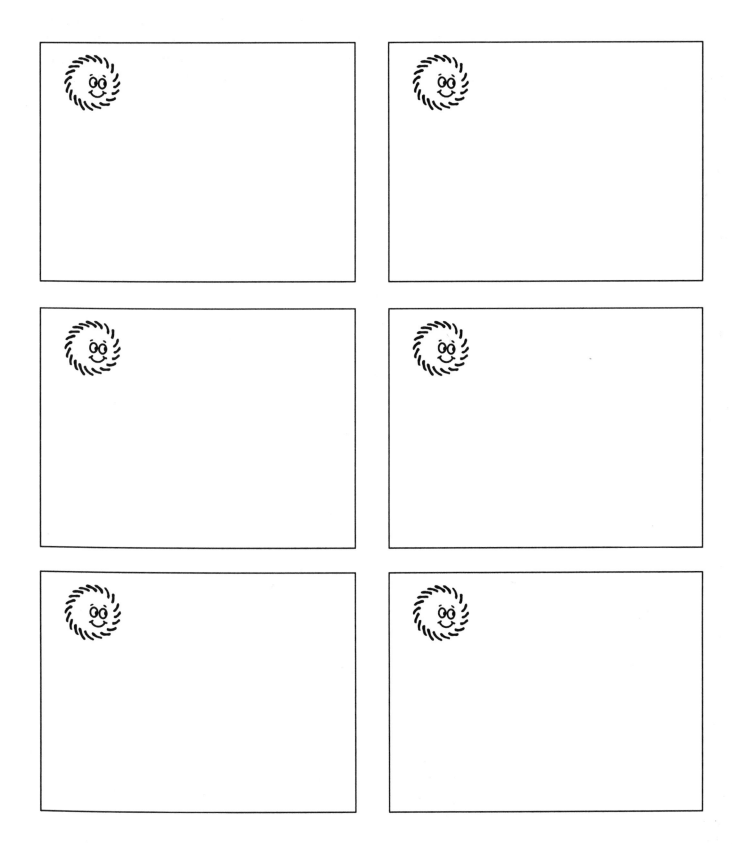

Walk the Line With Compliments or Put-Downs

Objective Students will discover how positive and negative comments affect performance.

Materials String or yarn at least 15 feet long

Procedure This activity is an almost magical demonstration of how much more effective positive comments are than negative remarks when someone is trying to do something difficult.

Tell students that you'd like to show them the difference between getting put-downs or getting compliments when they're trying to do something difficult.

Lay a long piece of string or yarn in a straight line on the floor. Ask for a student volunteer, and explain that his or her job will be to walk along this line keeping their feet on it with each step. The trick is, the volunteer will be blindfolded (be sure to use a blindfold that goes far enough down so that the person cannot see their feet or the ground.) Walk the blindfolded volunteer over to one end of the line.

Explain that the rest of the class will be guiding the volunteer. Divide the remaining class members into two groups. The first group will stand with equal numbers of students on both sides of the line, spread out from the volunteer to the middle of the string's length. The second group will stand in the same fashion from the midpoint to the end of the string.

Explain that the members of the first group will give positive and encouraging remarks or compliments to the volunteer as he or she walks along the first half of the line. They will say things like "You're doing great!" "That's it, you're right on the mark!" "Fantastic—keep going!" and "Hey, that's perfect—your foot is right on the line!" Tell the students not to actually guide or give directions; their job is to give compliments and encouragement. Only members of this first group are allowed to talk until the volunteer reaches the midpoint of the string.

Next, instruct the second group. This group will give only negative comments and put-downs as the person walks along their part of the line. They will say things like "You're clumsy—you can't even walk straight!" "Can't you do any better than that? What a joke!" "Look, she can't even get two steps in a row right!" "You'll never get back on the line—why don't you just give up?" and "Look he's walking toward the door! Ha, ha, ha!" When the volunteer walks this last part of the line, only members of the second group are allowed to speak.

Finally, select two students to count the number of times the volunteer's feet touch the line. These students will follow along with the volunteer. One student will count for the first half of the line when positive comments are being given, and the other will count when the volunteer walks along the second half of the line.

Tell the volunteer to start walking. Give the same kinds of positive and negative comments yourself as the volunteer walks, to keep the two groups focused on their tasks. Have the volunteer stop and take off his or her blindfold when he or she has veered way off from the string or has reached its end. Usually the volunteer will begin to veer off markedly soon after he or she reaches the negative comments half of the walk.

Repeat the process with other volunteers. Help students see the correlation between positive or negative comments and how they affect performance.

How to Accept a Compliment

Objective   Students will respond appropriately, using three specific steps, when receiving a compliment from their peers.

Materials   Lesson 6, Transparency #3, "Steps for Giving a Compliment," and Transparency #4, "Every Person Is a Mix of Things You Like and Don't Like

Transparency #1 - "Compliment Survey"

Transparency #2 - "Accepting a Compliment"

Transparency #3 - "Steps for Accepting a Compliment"

Handout #1 - "What to Say When You Receive a Compliment"

Handout #2 - "Compliment Role-Plays," one set of role-plays cut into cards (one for each pair of Learning Partners)

Scissors for each student

Wet cloth for erasing transparencies

Beanbag, Kushball™ or soft object for throwing (or Warm Fuzzy to toss, as described in the Variation at end of this lesson)

To the Teacher

An obstacle to giving and receiving compliments is that many of us have been programmed to believe that it is immodest to acknowledge a compliment and that the proper response to a compliment is to deny it. Denying or refusing a compliment makes the giver uncomfortable.

Children with low self-esteem often reject compliments because they think the giver isn't sincere, is trying to trick them, or wants something. Children from cultures where modesty is highly valued may find it especially difficult to accept a compliment. It may take these children some time to feel comfortable receiving praise from their peers.

In this lesson, students will learn how to acknowledge compliments and will practice both giving and receiving compliments with ease and grace.

If you are using this curriculum in a grade-level format, the following are the suggested grade-level Supplementary Activities for you to use to reinforce lesson concepts. "The Warm Fuzzy Game" is particularly valuable in providing students with practice in giving and receiving compliments.

1st   "A Compliment Web"
           (Supplementary Activity #1)

2nd   "Class Friend"
           (Supplementary Activity #2)
           "Compliment and Thank You Notes"
           (Supplementary Activity #3)

3rd   "The Warm Fuzzy Game"
           (Supplementary Activity #4)

Lesson Presentation

**Lesson 6,
Transp. #3
Transp. #4**

Remind students of the previous lesson and the fact that the class has been working on making their classroom a "warm, fuzzy" place to be through complimenting each other. You may wish to read a few of the Fuzzy-Grams you've received since Lesson 6 or invite students to share some of theirs. Review Lesson 6, Transparency #3, "Steps for Giving a Compliment," and Transparency #4, "Every Person Is a Mix of Things You Like and Don't Like." Ask for volunteers to give a classmate a compliment and demonstrate the three steps. (You may also want to review the four kinds of compliments listed on Transparency #6 from Lesson 6, "Compliments: Sentence Starters and Words," if volunteers aren't modeling a variety of compliments.)

THE AWKWARDNESS OF RECEIVING A COMPLIMENT

Say or paraphrase: **I think we're doing a good job in our class of learning to give each other compliments. That's a very important step in creating a warm, fuzzy environment in our room. Let me tell you about another classroom in another town that was learning to give compliments. They were getting really good at doing it—just like you—but there was one thing missing. Listen to the story and see if you can figure out what it is:**

> Tom and Dave had been learning to give compliments in their room at school. One day everyone was putting away their things after art. As Tom was putting away his markers, he happened to notice the picture that Dave had made. It was really good! Now Tom didn't know Dave very well, but he'd learned that when you have a nice thought about someone else, that's a good time to give them a compliment. So Tom walked over to Dave's desk, admired his picture, and said, "Dave, I think your picture is really great!" Dave kind of looked down at the floor and said, "Naw—it's not very good. See, I smudged it over here." and he pointed to a small smudge in the corner.

Discuss the story with the class. Ask questions like the following: **Dave wasn't trying to be rude; why do you think he responded the way he did? How do you think he felt? How do you think Tom felt when Dave reacted to his compliment that way? Do you think what Dave did and said encouraged or discouraged Tom in trying to be friendly? Have you ever complimented someone and had them say something negative about themselves in return, or tell you they thought that the compliment wasn't really true?** *Allow for student response.*

Many of us feel uncomfortable when someone says something nice about us. Sometimes we don't know what to say back. Did any of you have that experience this past week when we were practicing giving compliments? Did anyone find yourself not knowing what to say? *Allow for student response.*

It's not unusual for us to feel awkward and embarrassed when someone gives us a compliment. Just for the fun of it, let's take a survey and see how most of us feel and act when we receive a compliment.

Transp. #1

Place Transparency #1, "Compliment Survey," on the overhead, covering it with a sheet of paper. **First let's talk about what we think to ourselves or how we feel when someone gives us a compliment. When I read aloud, I want you to ask yourself, "Does this happen to me a <u>lot</u>?" If it happens to you often when someone says something nice to you, then raise your hand. I'll raise my hand, too. I'll count the hands and write down the number of us who have this feeling a lot. Are you ready?**

Move down the first half of the questionnaire, uncovering one feeling-related item at a time. Write in any other feelings students indicate they often have. Next, move to the bottom half of the transparency and tabulate agreements on how students act. After the survey is completed, review the results with the class, noting which thoughts and behaviors are the most common. Stress how common it is to feel awkward when we receive compliments.

Transp. #2

This survey proves it! We all feel uncomfortable sometimes when we get a compliment. Maybe we're all so accustomed to getting Cold Pricklies that we don't know what to do when we get a Warm Fuzzy! Anyway, we know how Dave felt in our story. *Put Transparency #2, "Accepting a Compliment," on the overhead; draw a turned-down mouth on the face.* **Maybe Dave was thinking, "I don't really deserve this compliment!"** *Write this in one of the bubbles above the boy's head.* **Or maybe he thought, "Tom will think I'm bragging about my picture if I act like I liked the compliment," or "Tom doesn't really mean it!"** *Write "I'm bragging" or "He didn't really mean it" in the second bubble.* **Or maybe Dave is just really embarrassed and wishes Tom would just please shut up!** *Write, "I'm embarrassed!" in the third bubble. (You may alter these comments to reflect the items that received the most votes in your class survey.)*

THE IMPORTANCE OF ACCEPTING A COMPLIMENT

Knowing how to accept a compliment is just as important as knowing how to give a compliment. A compliment is like a free ticket to feel <u>good</u> about ourselves, and we don't want to throw it away. You wouldn't throw away a free ticket to a movie or a skating rink, would you? Knowing what to do and say when we get a compliment can help us enjoy them more. And—guess what?—it makes it more fun for the person who gives us the compliment, too. So, when we learn how to accept a compliment, we can make two people happy: ourselves and the person who's complimenting us!

THREE STEPS FOR ACCEPTING A COMPLIMENT

Transp. #3

Put Transparency #3, "Steps for Accepting a Compliment," on the overhead; cover it. **Just as there were three steps to giving a compliment, there are also three small steps to take when we want to <u>accept</u> someone's compliment. I'll bet if I asked you to guess, you could figure them all out, but I'll show them to you just the same.**

The first one is—*uncover step #1***—to LOOK at the person. Why would you want to look at the person? Why is that important?** *Allow for student response.* **We look at someone when they talk to us because it means we're listening to them. They know we are hearing them.**

Uncover step #2. **While you're looking at the person, you THANK the person. When you thank someone, you let them know that you like it that they're nice enough to take the time to give you a compliment. Don't worry that you're bragging when you accept the compliment they give you. When someone else likes something about you, it's not bragging for you to thank them for telling you.**

Uncover step #3. **The last step is to let yourself FEEL GOOD about the compliment. At first, you can just feel good that someone liked what you did enough to tell you about it. Then, think about what it is they said they like about you. Let their compliment "sink in"—let it make you feel good and warm inside. Don't just shrug it off and tell yourself the person didn't mean it or it's not true. Don't close it out; <u>let it sink in and make you feel good</u>!**

Transp. #2

Erase Transparency #2 and put it back on the overhead. **Here's Dave again. This time he's going to follow the three steps and accept Tom's compliment.** <u>*Draw a smiling mouth on Dave.*</u> **Now, what's the first thing Dave's going to do?** *Allow for student response.* **What's the second step?** *Allow for student response.* **And the third step?** *Allow for student response.* **What are some things Dave could say to Tom to let Tom know he is accepting the compliment?** *Allow for student response; help students brainstorm possible responses like "Thanks; Thank you; I'm glad you like it; I appreciate the compliment; I'm glad you think so; It's nice of you to say so"; etc. Write the responses in the three bubbles on the transparency.*

Handout #1

We're going to practice receiving compliments, so I'm going to give you a list of things you can say when someone compliments you. *Distribute Handout #1, "What to Say When You Receive a Compliment." Go over the list with students and tell them to circle the responses they particularly like. Ask them to have one of their choices be more than just saying "Thanks." Have them keep the handouts nearby during the practice exercises which follow. Then have them put them in their Friendship Folders.*

MODELING THE THREE STEPS

Transp. #3

Put Transparency #3, "Steps for Accepting a Compliment," back on the overhead. **Would anyone like to be my Learning Partner for a minute and help me in a role-play? My Partner will give me a compliment, and I'll follow the three steps for accepting the compliment. I will Look, Thank, and Feel Good. In class today, when we do the Feel Good step we'll just say, "I let it sink in" or "I let myself believe it" to show that we let the compliment sink in and make us feel good.**

My Partner can compliment me on something I'm wearing or on the way I look. I'll help you if you get stuck. *Choose a student and guide him or her in giving you a compliment. Model the three steps of receiving the compliment.*

Thanks for being my Learning Partner. Let's try it again. This time I'll leave out one of the steps. You see if you can tell me which one I left out. Who would like to be my next Learning Partner? *Call on other students to give you different types of compliments (behavior, skill, belongings) and respond by omitting one of the steps each time. Ask students to identify the omitted step. In your incorrect modeling, include deflecting the compliment in some manner: deny it, give yourself a put-down, or ignore it. Ask your Learning Partner how they felt when you didn't accept their compliment.*

STUDENTS ROLE-PLAY GIVING AND RECEIVING COMPLIMENTS

Handout #2

I think you're getting the hang of it! Let's have a couple of volunteers to play both parts. I have a stack of role-play cards here. *Indicate stack of cards from Handout #2, "Compliment Role Plays."* **One of you will draw a card, think about it a minute, and then give the other one a compliment. Then the second person will follow the three steps for receiving the compliment — Look, Thank, and Feel Good. Who'd like to be first?**

Choose pairs of students to role-play giving and receiving compliments. Encourage the students to take a moment to think about their responses. Point out correct examples, reinforcing students' efforts and/or making suggestions for improvements. Have the students reverse roles and draw another card, or choose another pair of volunteers. There are two blank cards on the handout for you to add scenarios relevant to your classroom.

After several students have role-played giving and receiving compliments, say or paraphrase: **You're doing such a good job, I think you can all practice now with your Learning Partners. Decide with your partner who is the shortest. The shortest person will be A and the one who is taller will be B. Who is an A? — raise your hand. Who is a B?**

Now, I'm going to give each pair of Learning Partners a sheet of role-plays. Bs, will you cut the sheet in half and give half to A? Thanks. Now, I'd like both of you to cut out your role-play cards and spread them on the table where both of you can see them. *Allow time for cutting.*

Now, As, I want you to choose one of the role-plays you especially like; then, Bs, you choose one. *Have students take turns choosing their favorite scenarios until each student has chosen three or four.*

Now, A, read your first card to yourself. *Pause.* **O.K., As, give B a compliment. Be sure to look B in the eye and say your compliment like you mean it.** *Pause.* **Now, Bs, follow the three steps on the overhead for accepting A's compliment.** *Pause.* **Good! As, tell B if it looked to you like he or she followed the three steps for accepting a compliment — Look, Thank, and Feel Good.** *Pause.* *Have students take turns using their role-plays to give compliments;*

encourage the complimented student to refer to Handout #1, "What to Say When You Receive a Compliment," and to follow the three steps on the overhead. Have students give feedback to each other regarding whether they each followed the three steps for giving and receiving compliments. Walk around the room, monitoring student responses.

PRACTICING IN A COMPLIMENT CIRCLE

As I walked around the room, I heard so many good compliments! So many good ways of saying "Thank you!" I'd like us to play a complimenting game all together in a big circle. *Have students join you in a circle on the floor.*

I'm going to throw the beanbag *(Kushball™/Warm Fuzzy/etc.)* **to someone in the circle and give them a compliment. It can be any kind of compliment. The person who catches this will follow the three steps and accept my compliment. It will go like this.** *Throw the beanbag to a student and give him or her a compliment. (If you're concerned about a particular student who you predict may be left until last, throw the beanbag to that student yourself when you begin the activity.) Encourage the receiving student to pause a moment and let the compliment sink in; remind him or her to Look, Thank, and Feel Good.*

To the student catching the beanbag: **Good job. Now, YOU throw it to another person and give them a compliment. They will <u>look</u> you in the eye, <u>thank</u> you for the compliment, and say something that shows they <u>feel good</u> about the compliment. One other rule: you can't throw the beanbag to someone who has already caught it, it has to go to someone new.**

Encourage students to watch closely when someone receives a compliment to see if that person is really letting the compliment "sink in" or if the compliment seems to be "bouncing off" the person. When a student looks embarrassed upon receiving a compliment, encourage him or her to absorb the compliment and to feel good inside because of it.

Students may throw the beanbag to whomever they wish. Everyone will get a turn since the beanbag cannot be thrown to anyone twice. (This activity is so reinforcing and nurturing for students that they generally ask if they can have the circle again. You may wish to have the Compliment Circle as a recurring activity in your room.)

VARIATIONS

- *You can make a Warm Fuzzy toss to use in place of the beanbag by gluing small pieces of long-pile fur cloth onto the outer surface of a tennis ball. Part the fur and glue movable eyes from a craft supply store to the inner surface. You could also use a small fuzzy stuffed animal or a Kushball™.*

- *You may wish to write several sentence starters on a chart to prompt students as they practice giving compliments, such as:*
    - *I really like the way you . . . .*
    - *You're really good at . . . .*
    - *I think you're . . . .*
    - *The thing I like best about you is . . . .*
    - *I think you would be good at . . . .*
  They can also refer to Handout #1 ("Compliments: Sentence Starters and Words") and Handout #2 ("Fuzzy-Gram") from the last lesson.

LESSON REVIEW

A number of Supplementary Activities follow the lesson to provide opportunities for students to practice giving and receiving compliments. "The Warm Fuzzy Game" is an especially fun way for students to practice being the giver and recipient of compliments, as well as practice in responding to put-downs in a nonaggressive manner.

Compliment Survey

When someone gives you a compliment, what do you feel or think?

_____   Do you think the person is lying?

_____   Do you feel embarrassed?

_____   Do you think they're just saying it because they want
something from you?

_____   Do you feel happy?

_____   Do you feel friendly towards that person?

_____   Do you wonder what to say?

When you give others a compliment, how do they usually act?

_____   Do they give a compliment right back?

_____   Do they change the subject?

_____   Do they say that it isn't really true?

_____   Do they put themselves down?

_____   Do they look down or pretend they didn't hear it?

_____   Do they smile?

_____   Do they look pleased and say,
"Thanks"?

_____   Do they _____?

TRANSPARENCY #2

Accepting a Compliment

Steps for Accepting a Compliment

1.

LOOK
at the person.

2.

THANK
the person.

3.

FEEL GOOD—
let the compliment "sink in."

What to Say When You Receive a Compliment

- "Hey, thanks!"

- "That's nice of you to tell me."

- "Thank you. I've been working on that a long time" (if you get a compliment on something you've learned to do).

- "Thanks for telling me."

- "I appreciate you telling me that."

- "Thanks! That makes me feel good."

- "Thanks, I really like it too" (when you get a compliment on something you have, you own, or you are wearing).

- "Thanks, . . ." (and then tell him or her something about it— for example:) "I got it for my birthday."

HANDOUT #2

Compliment Role-Plays

Your friend has a new haircut.	Your friend did well on a big test in a subject that's been really hard for him or her.
Your friend got the highest score in class on a test.	The kid sitting next to you isn't a good friend of yours, but you see that he or she did really well on a writing assignment.
Your teacher helped you get through an embarrassing moment without the other kids noticing.	Your friend convinced you to try a new snack and you really liked it.
Your friend lent you some money.	Your friend has offered to help you clean up your yard.
Your friend helped you to figure out a tough math problem.	You think your friend's new jacket really looks great.
Your dad finally got promoted at work after not getting it his last two tries.	Your friend drew a picture you don't really like. Still, you want to say something to make your friend feel good.
Your mother has been really listening to you lately and you want to tell her how much you appreciate it.	Your friend has a really terrific bike.

A Compliment Web

Objective   Students will practice giving and receiving compliments to and from each other while passing a ball of string around the circle.

Materials   Ball of string or yarn

Procedure   Have the class or a smaller group sit in a circle on the floor. Tell the class they're going to make a web by playing a compliment game. Remind them of the steps for giving and receiving a compliment.

Hold one end of the string and carry the rest of the ball to a student in the circle and model giving the student a compliment. Help the student to model receiving the compliment. That student then holds the string and carries the ball to another student, letting out enough slack so that the string continues from you to him or her and then to the third student. Each student passes the ball of string to another, giving a compliment and continuing to hold the string. As the ball is passed around the circle to every student a "web" will form.

You may wish to untangle the web using the same compliment practice while rolling the string back onto the ball.

Class Friend

Objective   The students will learn to reinforce positive behaviors in their peers by observing each other's behaviors and making specific compliments regarding them.

Materials   Blank transparency and pen
Jar or container with slips of paper containing names of students
Class Friend Badge (Supplementary Activity #2 Materials)
4" x 3" pin style name badge (convention size)
Yarn, index cards, colored pens

Procedure   Tell the class that they will all be getting a chance to practice the friendship skills they have been learning by being the "Class Friend" for a day. (You may wish to use transparencies from previous lessons and discuss the friendship skills students have been learning.)

Tell students that each day one of their names will be drawn from the name jar; that person will be the official Class Friend for the day and wear the Class Friend Badge. The Class Friend will try especially hard all day to practice good friendship skills. During that day the rest of the class will notice the friendly, helpful behavior of the Class Friend and be ready with some compliments. At the end of the day, model for the class by giving the Class Friend a compliment on his or her friendly behavior. Call on several students to give the Class Friend compliments, encouraging them to be specific, such as "I liked it when you . . . ." Write these compliments on a transparency; transfer them to index cards tied to a piece of yarn for the Class Friend to take home and hang in his or her bedroom. (You may wish to select a student to copy compliments from the transparency onto the cards with colored pens.)

After each compliment, the Class Friend uses the skills from this lesson and thanks his or her complimenter. The Class Friend draws a new name from the name jar to be the Class Friend the next day. You may wish to designate two of three Class Friends each day; this way students don't have to wait so long to have their turns and the complimenting skills are still fresh in their memories.

Class Friend Badge

Color the star silver or gold. Cut out, and insert in a 4" x 3" pin style name badge (convention size).

Compliment and Thank You Notes

Objective   Students will practice giving and receiving compliments by writing notes to each other.

Materials   Compliment and Thank You Notes (Supplementary Activity #3 Handout) duplicated
Lidded box with slit in top
Class list cut up and placed in jar or sack

Procedure   Tell students you have provided them with some special notes so they can practice giving and receiving compliments. Encourage students to write at least one long sentence or two short ones, so as to avoid notes that are too short, such as "I like your hair!" or "Thank you." Suggest a format of "I like _____ because . . ." or something similar, as well as a response that shows they read the Compliment Note, such as "Thank you for saying . . . ."

Provide students with a stack of Compliment Notes and Thank You Notes near a "mailbox." From time to time, assign students a person to write a compliment to. You can do this either by having students draw names or by whispering the name of the student two places below their name in your grade-book. Have students put their compliments in the classroom mailbox. At the end of the day, choose a couple of students to deliver the notes in the mailbox. Allow students sufficient time to write Thank You Notes and deliver them.

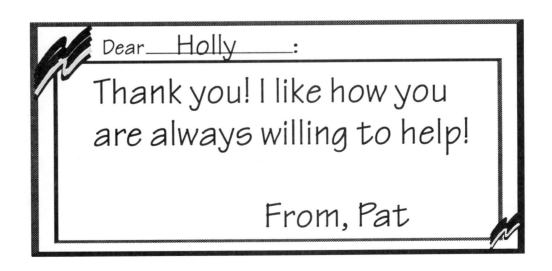

VARIATION

You may give students suggestions on who to write compliments to, such as "Write a compliment to:

- Someone you don't know very well."
- Someone taller than you."
- Someone shorter than you."
- Someone who sits far away from you."
- The person who sits behind you."
- Your Learning Partner."

Compliment and Thank You Notes

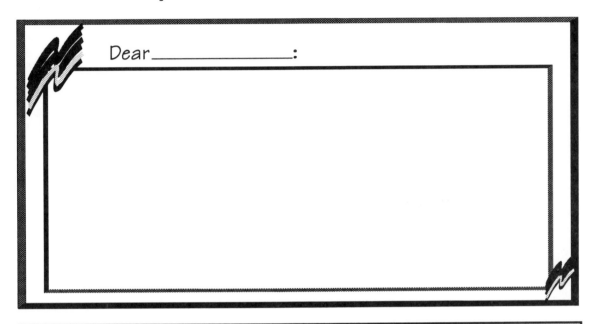

Dear _____:

I think you're neat because . . .

I like you because . . .

The Warm Fuzzy Game

Objective   Students will learn to give and receive
compliments and to respond appropriately to put-downs.

Materials   "The Warm Fuzzy Game" boards (Supplementary Activity #4 Game,
Parts One and Two)

Game instructions

Game Score Sheet (Supplementary Activity #4 Score Sheets)

Warm Fuzzies (run on yellow or pink paper) (Supplementary Activity
#4 Warm Fuzzies Sheet)

Cold Pricklies (run on blue paper) (Supplementary Activity #4 Cold
Pricklies Sheet)

Warm Fuzzy and Cold Prickly Cards (Supplementary Activity #4
Game Card Sheets #1-#8)

A marker for each player

Response Cards (Supplementary Activity #4 Response Cards)

One puppet, preferably mean- or ugly-looking

Procedure   The Warm Fuzzy Game is a wonderful way for students to practice
giving compliments and handling put-downs assertively. The purpose
of the game is for students to give as many Warm Fuzzies (compliments)
as possible and to banish Cold Pricklies (put-downs). You can set the
game up as a learning center and have students play in small groups
(of from three to six) at different times during the day. It's even more
fun, however, to have students help you make up enough games so that
everyone in the class can play at once.

ASSEMBLING THE GAME BOARD

The game board can be assembled by simply taping copies of the two
pages of the game together. Once you've made the game board, it can
then be colored and covered with clear contact paper or laminated.

OBJECT OF THE GAME

The purpose of this game is for students to practice giving and receiving compliments and responding appropriately to put-downs. Students should try to give away as many Warm Fuzzies as they can and send back ("banish") as many Cold Pricklies as possible to Cold Prickly Land. The best strategy to win the game is to be nice to other people and help them get rid of their Cold Pricklies.

GAME CONTENTS

(For **four** players; if more play add game materials as indicated below.)

- 48 Warm Fuzzies
- 24 Cold Pricklies
- Warm Fuzzy and Cold Prickly Cards (Supplementary Activity #4 Game Card Sheets #1-#8)
- 4 markers, 2 dice
- 4 Response Cards (Supplementary Activity #4 Response Cards)
- 1 puppet to use when giving Cold Pricklies

(For each additional player, add 12 Warm Fuzzies, 6 Cold Pricklies, 1 marker, and 1 score sheet.)

HOW TO PLAY

A complete game consists of all players traveling around the game board one time. They may go around more than once if desired, but everyone will have plenty of chances to give and receive Warm Fuzzies in just one round.

Each player should choose a colored marker and twelve Warm Fuzzies. Players may keep their Warm Fuzzies in a pile near them until they have a chance to give them away. At the start, all Cold Pricklies should be left in a game box, which should be sitting near the game board.

To begin, place all markers on the "START HERE" square. Put the Warm Fuzzy cards and Cold Prickly cards face down on their respective squares on the game board. Throw the dice to determine who goes first; the player who has the highest number begins the game.

The first player throws the dice and moves his or her marker as many squares as indicated on both dice. The player on the right has the next turn. Rolling "doubles" (both dice the same number) does not give any extra turn.

Along the path there are five kinds of squares:

1. SHADED SQUARES: When you land here nothing happens. Play goes to the next person.

2. WARM FUZZY SQUARES: When you land on a Warm Fuzzy Square you receive a compliment. This is done as follows:

   a. The person on your left will give you one of his or her Warm Fuzzies.

   b. That person then draws a Warm Fuzzy Card from the pile and reads it to you.

   c. Looking at the reader, you will then respond to the compliment, using the suggestions on your Response Card if you wish.

   d. When done, BOTH you and the person on your left SCORE 2 POINTS.

3. COLD PRICKLY SQUARES: When you land on a Cold Prickly Square, you'll have to respond to a put-down. The person on your left will hand you a Cold Prickly from the game box and then use the puppet to read aloud the next Cold Prickly Card drawn from the stack. You will then choose a response from your Response Card, look at the puppet, and respond to the put-down (saying, for example, "No matter what you say, I'm still an O.K. person!") When you give a good response like this to a put-down, you SCORE 1 POINT.

   Keep any Cold Pricklies you get out in front of you, where other players can see them and banish them.

4. DETOUR SQUARES: These squares give you a choice to continue around the board or to try to help someone get rid of a Cold Prickly.

5. BANISH! SQUARES: These squares are only available if you "go out of your way" by taking the detours. Landing on a Banish! Square lets you do two things: First, you get to take away someone else's Cold Prickly! Choose the nearest player on your left who has a Cold Prickly. Take the Cold Prickly and say "I hereby banish this to Cold Prickly Land forever!" as you put it into the Cold Prickly Land space on the game board. Next, the second thing you will do is to give that same person a compliment. Read to him or her the next Warm Fuzzy Card from the stack, and give out one of your Warm Fuzzies. (The person should respond to your compliment, but this time he or she doesn't score any points for doing so.)

Because banishing Cold Prickly put-downs and giving compliments are such great things to do, SCORE 5 POINTS for yourself.

NOTE: If no one else has any Cold Pricklies, you may then banish one of your own. Score only 3 points in this case. If no one at all has Cold Pricklies, then treat this the same as if you landed on a Shaded Square.

As the game progresses everyone will receive both Warm Fuzzies and Cold Pricklies. Since Cold Pricklies hurt, the object of the game is to banish as many as possible of these put-downs to Cold Prickly Land. Whenever players see that some of the other players are getting a lot of Cold Pricklies, they can help the other person out (and get extra points for themselves) by "going out of their way" on the detour routes to try to land on a Banish! Square.

The game is over when the LAST player reaches "START HERE" again. All players then add up their points, adding an extra point for any Warm Fuzzies they have and subtracting one point for any Cold Pricklies they still hold. Declare the player with the most points as the official "winner," but remind students that really everyone who gives compliments and reduces put-downs is a winner!

Sample Game

NOTE: This is what the game board will look like. The following two pages of the game can be enlarged and laminated for student use.

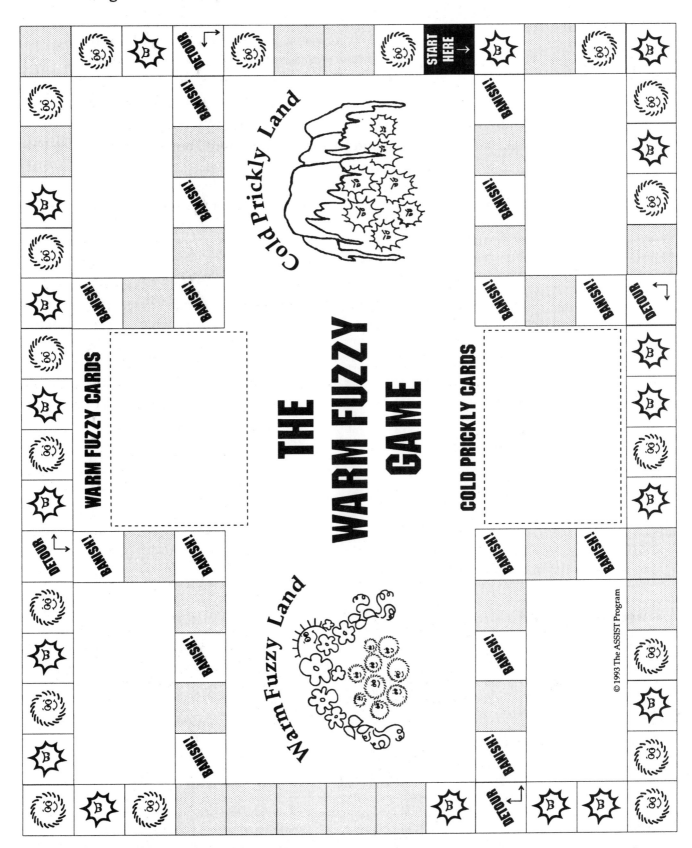

WARM FUZZ

Warm Fuzzy Land

TH
WARM I
GAI

COLD PRICKI

DETOUR

BANISH!

© 1993 The ASSIST Program

UZZY CARDS

BANISH!

BANISH!   BANISH!   BANISH!   DETOUR

Cold Prickly Land

HE FUZZY ME

CKLY CARDS

BANISH!   BANISH!   BANISH!

BANISH!   DETOUR

START HERE

Warm Fuzzy Cards

I think you have good ideas!

I think you're really clever.

You are a good listener.

You're fun to be with.

I like the way you really pitch in and help when there's a job to do!

I like doing things with you.

I think you're generous.

You're a good sport!

I think you can be depended on.

Warm Fuzzy Cards

I like your hair.	Your're nice.	You look nice today!
I like your honesty!	You look great!	You really work hard.
I think you are a friendly person!	I like the way you think of other people's feelings.	You're so organized!

Warm Fuzzy Cards

You seem like the kind of person who is generous with your things.

I bet you share your things when you play with your friends.

I bet if you had a pet you would take really good care of it!

You're wearing nice colors today!

I bet your friends have fun when you're around.

I like the way you share!

What you say in class is really interesting.

I bet you are brave when things get scary.

I bet if somebody got hurt you would try to help them.

Warm Fuzzy Cards (to fill in yourself)

Cold Prickly Cards

Aren't you a little early for Halloween?	Yo, Squid Body!	You're so stupid you'll probably flunk recess.
Your mother sure dresses you funny!	Nice outfit—did the thrift store have a sale?	You're such a klutz!
If I had a face like yours, I'd walk backwards!	Do you take ugly pills, or what?	Hey, Cucumber Nose!

Cold Prickly Cards

What a motor-mouth!	What a dumb-looking outfit!	Do you take dork lessons or does it just come naturally?
Your name should be Garbage Mouth—you'll eat anything!	Hey, Lizard Lips—you even scare monsters.	You look better—did you have plastic surgery?
The last time I saw a nose like yours, it was on a snowman.	Get lost, Oyster Brain.	You walk like a duck! Quack! Quack!

Cold Prickly Cards

Weird shirt! Are you starting a new style for preschoolers?	Did you comb your hair with an eggbeater?	Nice move, Klutz—you can't even walk without tripping!
Hey, Geek—is that a mask or your face?	You always wreck everything!	You're so ugly you have to sneak up on a mirror.
You never get anything right, Beetle Brain!	Bug off, Banana Nose!	Are those your Grandma's shoes?

Cold Prickly Cards (to fill in yourself)

Warm Fuzzies

SUPPLEMENTARY ACTIVITY #4 COLD PRICKLIES SHEET

Cold Pricklies

Response Cards

What to say when you get a compliment:

- "Thanks!"

- "Thank you. I've been working on that a long time."

- "Thanks for telling me."

- "Thanks, I like it, too" (for a compliment on what you're wearing or something you own).

- "Thanks, . . ." (and then tell them something about it—for example:) "I got it for my birthday."

- "It makes me feel good to hear that."

What to say when you get a put-down:

- "Wish you wouldn't worry about me so much!"

- "Has this been bothering you for long?"

- "That was supposed to be a secret."

- "Amazing, but true."

- "I thought you'd never notice!"

- "Oh no, really?"

- "Gee you're nice."

- "Would you put that in writing?"

- "See my lawyer."

THE WARM FUZZY GAME

—S C O R E   S H E E T—

Name _____
Color of Marker _____

P O I N T S
Responding to a Cold Prickly = 1 pt.
Giving a Warm Fuzzy = 2 pts.
Responding to a Warm Fuzzy = 2 pts.
Banishing your own Cold Prickly = 3 pts.
Banishing someone else's Cold Prickly = 5 pts.

_____ _____ _____
_____ _____ _____
_____ _____ _____
_____ _____ _____
_____ _____ _____

THE WARM FUZZY GAME

—S C O R E   S H E E T—

Name _____
Color of Marker _____

P O I N T S
Responding to a Cold Prickly = 1 pt.
Giving a Warm Fuzzy = 2 pts.
Responding to a Warm Fuzzy = 2 pts.
Banishing your own Cold Prickly = 3 pts.
Banishing someone else's Cold Prickly = 5 pts.

_____ _____ _____
_____ _____ _____
_____ _____ _____
_____ _____ _____
_____ _____ _____

THE WARM FUZZY GAME

—S C O R E   S H E E T—

Name _____
Color of Marker _____

P O I N T S
Responding to a Cold Prickly = 1 pt.
Giving a Warm Fuzzy = 2 pts.
Responding to a Warm Fuzzy = 2 pts.
Banishing your own Cold Prickly = 3 pts.
Banishing someone else's Cold Prickly = 5 pts.

_____ _____ _____
_____ _____ _____
_____ _____ _____
_____ _____ _____
_____ _____ _____

THE WARM FUZZY GAME

—S C O R E   S H E E T—

Name _____
Color of Marker _____

P O I N T S
Responding to a Cold Prickly = 1 pt.
Giving a Warm Fuzzy = 2 pts.
Responding to a Warm Fuzzy = 2 pts.
Banishing your own Cold Prickly = 3 pts.
Banishing someone else's Cold Prickly = 5 pts.

_____ _____ _____
_____ _____ _____
_____ _____ _____
_____ _____ _____
_____ _____ _____

Making a New Friend

Objective
Students will learn to use a set of six steps for initiating a conversation with a peer they don't know.

Materials
Transparency #1 - "What's the New Kid Like?"

Transparency #2 - "Relax and Say Encouraging Things to Yourself"

Transparency #3 - "Say 'Hi' and Tell Your Name"

Transparency #4 - "Ask a Question About . . ."

Transparency #5 - "How to Get Them Talking"

Transparency #6 - "Tell Something About Yourself"

Transparency #7 - "Suggest You Do Something Together"

Transparency #8A/Handout #1A/Poster #1A and Transparency #8B/Handout #1B/Poster #2B - "How to Talk to Another Person"

Transparency #9 - "How to Make a New Friend"

Handouts #2A and #2B - "Starting a Conversation With Someone You Don't Know"

To the Teacher
Students often find that when they want to make friends with someone they have met for the first time, they feel shy and don't have the skills to initiate conversation. This lesson teaches students how to overcome their sense of shyness with positive self-talk and basic conversation skills.

A simple six-step formula to "break the ice" will be taught. The purpose of these steps is to structure an information exchange so that students can uncover similarities. Students are more likely to progress toward friendship when they discover that they share things in common.

Through role-play, students learn to dialogue and to link their comments to the prior comments of the other person. They also learn to exchange information, find similarities, and establish common ground activities. Finally, students learn that if they think they might "hit it off" with another person, they will need to structure a time to get together again.

The Supplementary Activities for this lesson need to be adapted for nonreaders. All of these activities are appropriate for grades two through five. Supplementary Activity #1 looks at the possibility that sometimes students' efforts may not lead to friendships, and encourages students to take that eventuality in stride.

Lesson Presentation

Transp. #1

Say or paraphrase: **What if we got a new boy in our class today? What if when he came into our room, he said, "My name's Garth, and here's my Information Sheet . . ." and then he handed each one of you something that looked like this transparency.** *Put Transparency #1, "What's the New Kid Like?," on the overhead.*

Garth's Information Sheet tells us a lot of things about Garth. What are some of the things you could learn about him from his Sheet? *Allow for students to guess what the symbols mean. Students could learn that the new boy loves hamburgers, hates math, lives in an apartment building, that his family includes his mother and younger sister, that he likes to draw or do art, has a pet lizard named "Slither," plays soccer, and recently had a birthday and turned nine.* **We'd know a lot about this new kid, wouldn't we?**

O.K. Let's pretend we've finished reading Garth's Information Sheet. He says, "May I have <u>your</u> Information Sheets?" So let's pretend each one of you opens your folder and gives Garth your Information Sheet. What would Garth learn about you? What are some of the things your Information Sheet would say? *Ask students questions about the kinds of topics on Transparency #1.*

A lot of us would have something in common with Garth. It seems he would fit right into our class, doesn't it? Wouldn't it be great if we could <u>really</u> trade Information Sheets with people we didn't know? It would be SO EASY for us to get acquainted that way. It would be easy to know if someone new would be a good friend for us, wouldn't it?

IT'S NOT EASY TO START A CONVERSATION WITH SOMEONE WE DON'T KNOW

But new kids in our class don't come with Information Sheets, do they? If we want to get to know them, what do we have to do? How can we find out if they would make a good friend for us? *Allow for student response. Lead students to see that they will have to get their information by talking to a new person.*

Yes, if we want to find out what a new person is like, we're going to have to talk to them. We'll have to ask them questions about themselves, and we'll have to tell them about ourselves. That way, we'll find out if we have anything in common—if we want to make a friendship. **Can any of you remember a time when you started a conversation with someone you didn't know? How did it feel? Were you comfortable?** *Allow for student response. Encourage them to share their discomfort with initiating a conversation with strangers.*

Most of us feel shy when we talk to someone we don't know. But, if we don't go ahead and talk to the new person, we may miss a chance to make a new friend. Today we're going to learn some ways to put that nervousness aside and start conversations with someone we don't know.

STEP 1– R ELAX AND SAY ENCOURAGING THINGS TO YOURSELF

Transp. #2

When you see someone you don't know, and you think about talking to them, you may think, "Oh, no! I don't know what to say!" That's when you need to relax. Take a deep breath and tell yourself something positive. *Put Transparency #2, "Relax and Say Encouraging Things to Yourself," on the overhead.*

Tell yourself that the new person will be glad to have someone talk to him or her; tell yourself that you are good at being a friend; remind yourself that this is just another kid—not the President of the United States! **What are some other things you could say to encourage yourself when you're feeling shy about talking to a new kid?** *Allow for student response; you may wish to have students model by taking a deep breath before modeling their self-talk. Write some of their responses on the transparency.*

STEP 2 – SAY "HI" AND TELL YOUR NAME

Transp. #3

Good ideas! The important thing is to jump right in and DO IT! Just walk right up to the new person and say, "Hi. My name is ____"! *Put Transparency #3, "Say 'Hi' and Tell Your Name," on the overhead.* **And don't forget to . . .** *point to the smile on the transparency*

or model a big smile . . . **SMILE! What do you imagine the new person would think if you did this?** *Model saying, "Hi. My name is
_____."* *with a stern or uninterested look on your face.* **How do you think the new kid would feel if I greeted him or her like that?** *Allow for student response. Stress the importance of a friendly face being part of the communication.* **Yes, if we want a new kid to know we're being friendly, our faces have to be friendly, too.**

STEP 3–ASK AN OPEN-ENDED QUESTION

O.K. So you've taken a breath, reminded yourself that you can do this, walked up and introduced yourself with a smile. What do you think would be the next step? *Allow for student response.*

Transp. #4

Yes, you ask a question! This is the trick of talking to someone you don't know—asking questions! You don't have to think of things to say if you ask the new person questions about himself or herself. Probably the best question to ask first is, "What's your name?" After you've found out what the new kid's name is, there are lots of other things you can ask him or her about. *Put Transparency #4, "Ask a Question About . . .," on the overhead.* **Here are a few of the things you can ask about.** *Point to the various categories around the boys on the transparency, indicating they can ask questions about favorite sports, school, TV viewing, or favorite things to do. (You may have students formulate questions related to each topic.)* **These are just a few of the kinds of things you can ask. Can you think of others?** *Allow for student response (you may wish to refer to the questions in step #3 on Handout #1A, "How to Talk to Another Person"). Write students' questions at the bottom of the transparency.*

Some questions work better than others when you're trying to talk to someone. Let me show you what I mean. Would someone volunteer to pretend to be a new kid? *Choose a volunteer to answer questions. Whisper instructions to the volunteer to answer only with "Yes" or "No."* **Now, I'm going to try to start a conversation with this new kid by asking some questions.** *Ask the volunteer the following "Yes" or "No" questions:*

- **Are you new around here?**

- **Do you like our school?**

- **Are you in fourth grade?**
- **Do you like baseball?**

Well, I didn't seem to get anywhere. What happened? *Allow for student response. Help students see that questions that are answered "Yes" or "No" don't really help two people to talk together very well.*

When we ask questions that are answered with "Yes" or "No," it sounds more like a quiz than a conversation. It doesn't sound very friendly, does it? Will someone be my volunteer to answer a different kind of question? *Choose another volunteer; instruct the volunteer to answer the following questions:*

- **Where did you move from?**
- **What do you like about our school?**
- **Whose classroom are you in?**
- **What sports do you play?**

Why do these questions work better than the first ones? *Allow for student response.* **These are called "open-ended" questions, or "questions that get kids talking." They sound friendlier, don't they?**

Transp. #5

To help students practice distinguishing between open-ended and closed questions, show Transparency #5, "How to Get Them Talking." Take a piece of paper and cover all but the first "Yes" or "No" Question. Read this to students, then ask them what a better question might be, one that would provide more information than just "Yes" or "No." Accept students' responses, then lower the covering sheet to reveal another possible response that is open-ended and that could be used instead of the first question. Continue in this manner through the rest of the prepared questions on the transparency. Brainstorm with the class some other examples of closed and open-ended questions.

STEP 4–TELL SOMETHING ABOUT YOURSELF

Transp. #6

Using open-ended questions can help you with the next step in talking to someone you don't know. I'll show you how. *Put Transparency #6, "Tell Something About Yourself," on the overhead.* **As you are asking the new kid open-ended questions, you will want to tell him or her something about yourself, too. That's the only**

way you can both get to know each other. **What are some things you could tell a new kid about yourself that have to do with school?** *Allow for student response. Lead students to make statements that give information about what grade they're in, who their teacher is, what they like about their school, subjects they like or dislike, etc. Write some of the responses in the "school" bubble.*

Those would all be good things to tell someone who is just getting to know you. What could you tell the new kid about the movies you like or don't like? *Allow for students to respond about their movie preferences; write these responses in the "movies" bubble.*

Continue the exercise with the "TV shows" and "activities" bubbles. Use the last bubble for any miscellaneous information students think would help a new student in getting acquainted with them.

STEP 5–CONTINUE ASKING QUESTIONS AND TELLING ABOUT YOURSELF

This step is like playing a game of catch. You throw over a question and they toss you an answer back. Then you toss over some information about yourself. They might "throw the ball back" by asking you some questions or telling you some more about themselves.

STEP 6–SUGGEST YOU DO SOMETHING TOGETHER

Transp. #7

So, here you are, asking the new kid questions and telling him or her things about yourself. You're finding out ways you and the new kid are alike and ways you're different. If the kid seems like someone you might like for a friend, there's one more step to take. *Put Transparency #7, "Suggest You Do Something Together," on the overhead.* **You suggest that you and the new kid do something together. That will give you more time to get acquainted. You might ask the new kid to sit with you at lunch.** *Write "Would you like to sit with me at lunch?" in one of the bubbles on the transparency.* **What else could you ask?** *Encourage students to make up questions, such as: "Would you like to play together at recess?"; "Would you like to be on my team?"; "Would you like to come over after school?";*

"Do you want to help me make a poster for art?"; "Do you want to go to the ball game together?"; etc. and write them in the bubbles.

The best way to find out if you can be friends with someone is to spend time together. When you first meet someone, you're only getting a tiny slice of who they are. You're usually both a little nervous talking to each other the first time. It's important to give the other person a chance, and to get to know them better before you decide whether the two of you can be friends.

USING A VOLUNTEER TO MODEL THE SIX STEPS

The steps we've just talked about are not the ONLY ways to start a conversation with someone you don't know, but they're a good way to get started. So let's practice using them. I'd like to have a volunteer—I'll pretend to be the new kid, and I need someone who will start a conversation with me using the steps we've just gone through. *Choose a volunteer you think will model the six steps successfully.* **I'm going to give you each a handout that shows the six steps so you can help our volunteer if he or she needs it.**

**Handout #1A
Handout #1B
Transp. #8A**

Distribute copies of Handout #1A and #1B, "How to Talk to Another Person," run back-to-back. Put the transparency of the handout (Transparency #8A) on the overhead. Cover all but step #1.

Are you ready? Step #1 is what? *Have students identify the "relax" step and recall that relaxing can be accomplished by taking a deep breath and saying something encouraging to themselves. Encourage the volunteer to model relaxing and using encouraging self-talk.*

Good! Now, what is step #2? *Allow for student response. Have the volunteer model the second step. Call on help from other students, if necessary. Remind him or her to smile.*

That was a friendly greeting! *Uncover the third step.* **Now, what question do you want to ask me? There are some suggestions here on the overhead.** *Have the volunteer model asking an open-ended question. Ask the class if the question is open-ended or "Yes" or "No" to keep them involved in the process.*

That's a good question. It can't be answered by "Yes" or "No." Now it's my turn to answer. *Model answering the question.*

Transp. #8B *Put Transparency #8B on the overhead, covering all but step #4.* **Now it's your turn again. What do you do?** *The volunteer should remember to tell the "new kid" something about himself or herself.*

Now the conversation gets to be a little like a ping-pong game. *Uncover step #5 and read the step aloud.* **You'll continue asking me questions and telling me something about yourself.** *Read the questions and answers under step #5 on the transparency.* **Let's see if we can continue with questions and answers just like that.** *Encourage the volunteer to continue asking questions and giving information about himself or herself. Allow the class to offer examples of open-ended questions.*

After several questions, say: **By this time you're probably finding out if I would make a good friend for you. Let's pretend you think we could be friends. What's the last step in making conversation with a new kid?** *Uncover step #6 and have the volunteer read it aloud.* **Yes! You will want to suggest that we spend more time together. That way we can find out if we like to be together. What could you suggest?** *Have the volunteer formulate a question. Allow the class to offer suggestions, if necessary.*

PRACTICING THE SIX STEPS WITH LEARNING PARTNERS

That was fun! I want you all to get a chance to role-play. Let's practice with our Learning Partners. *Have students sit with their Learning Partners and decide who will be the "New Kid" and who will be the "Conversation Starter." Read the following scenarios to the class to set up the role-play, pausing to allow students time to create their characters. If they are asked for different kinds of information, tell them to make that up however they please.*

SCENARIO ONE

<u>New Kid</u>: **You just moved here from the state of _____. You played a sport there; you can decide what it was. You have two**

pets—one is an ordinary pet; the other is unusual; you decide, what they are. There's one thing you're very good at and one thing you're lousy at; you decide what those things are.

Conversation Starter: You've seen the new kid around for the past week. The new kid isn't in your class, so you haven't had a chance to find out anything about him or her. This is your chance to start a ping-pong conversation and find out if you two can be friends.

Guide students through the six steps on Transparencies #8A and #8B. Have the Learning Partners take turns being the New Kid and the Conversation Starter to role-play scenarios like the following:

SCENARIO TWO

New Kid: You've lived in this town all your life, but you just recently moved to this neighborhood. You decide what school you used to go to. Decide what your new teacher's name is and think of something that he or she does in his or her class that you especially like. You live somewhere other than in an ordinary house; you decide where you live.

Conversation Starter: You don't particularly like sports, but there is something else you're VERY good at; as a matter of fact, you're the best in your class. Decide what you're so good at. You're saving your money to buy a very special pet; decide what it is.

SCENARIO THREE

New Kid: You don't live around here. You're visiting your aunt for the summer. Your aunt doesn't have any kids and it gets kind of boring at her house. You've been spending a lot of time doing _____ (you decide) since there's no one to play with at your aunt's house. There's an activity you really like and are very good at, but you need someone else to play it with you; you decide what the activity is.

Conversation Starter: It's summer and you're a little bored because there aren't very many kids in your neighborhood. You've seen the new kid at the pool three times and you've decided to start a conversation to see if the two of you could be friends this summer.

SCENARIO FOUR

New Kid: You're visiting your cousin from another country; you decide where you're from. Your cousin is having a birthday party, and you don't know anyone there. You're really into music (you decide what kind). You brought a lot of tapes to play at the party but you have no one to talk to.

Conversation Starter: You're at your friend's birthday party. Your friend says, "Hey, come meet my cousin from out of town!" As soon as you walk over to this new person, your friend dashes off to answer the doorbell. You and your friend's cousin are just standing there, looking at each other and feeling weird.

WRITING A SCRIPT FOR CONVERSATION

Transp. #9

That was fun. You all did a good job keeping the conversation going. It doesn't matter if things stop; if it does, you just pick it up and start again, just like ping-pong. This conversation script reminds me of the game we were just playing. *Place Transparency #9, "How to Make a New Friend," on the overhead. Read the cartoon, or have students read it; ask students to identify what is happening in each step.*

We're going to practice being Conversation Starters this week. The more we practice, the easier it will be. Friendships don't just happen; someone has to get them started. When we gather up the courage to start a conversation with someone new, we increase our chances of having another person in our life to have fun with.

I want you to think right now of a specific time this week when you'll use what we've learned today. I'll be checking with you each day to see whether you've had a chance to use the six steps.

**Handout #2A
Handout #2B**

Use Handouts #2A and #2B, "Starting a Conversation With Someone You Don't Know," as an in-class or homework assignment. Instruct students to write conversations and responses appropriate to the six steps. Suggest they use Handouts #1A and #1B for reference. (You may wish to enlarge Handouts #1A and #1B and display them as posters in the classroom.)

The six steps taught in this lesson are not the only way students can initiate conversations with someone they don't know. However, it is always best for students to learn one thing to master, rather than being exposed to a number of techniques while learning none of them well. After students have become comfortable using the six steps in this lesson, you may wish to broaden their conversation skills by suggesting that they also can initiate conversations by stating an opinion ("The P.E. teacher sure is nice."), giving a compliment ("I really like your jacket."), or stating a fact ("Boy! It sure is raining hard!"). You may also tell students that one of the best ways they can learn to make friends is to watch others who are friendly and to figure out what they do that works so well.

LESSON REVIEW

Use the Supplementary Activities to provide additional practice of the skills taught in this lesson.

TRANSPARENCY #1

What's the New Kid Like?

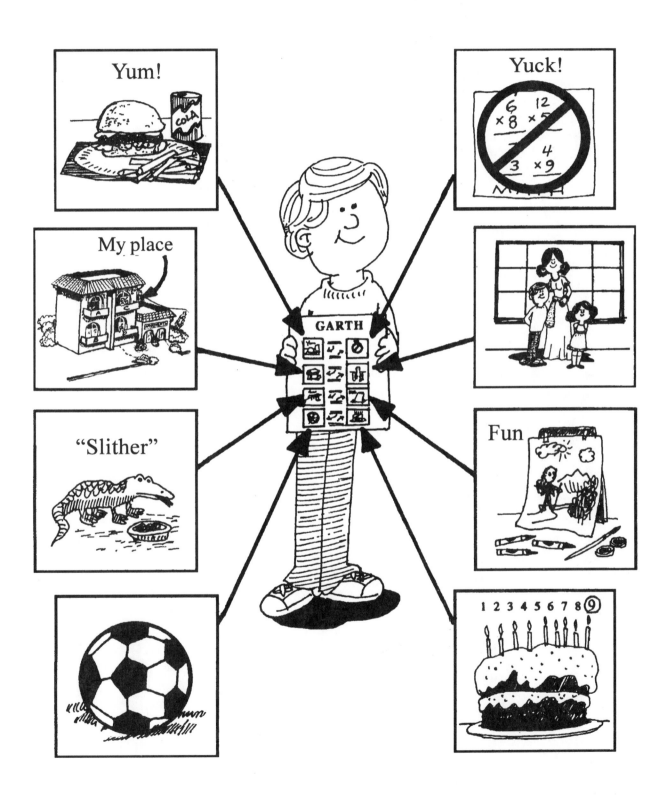

Relax and Say Encouraging Things to Yourself

Other things you can say to yourself:

- "I'm fun to play with and people like me. This kid will, too."

- "I like meeting new people and can think of good things to say to them."

- "I feel shy, but I can do it."

- "This kid might be shy and really want a new friend."

- "Maybe it'll work out, maybe it won't—I can handle whatever happens."

- "If this person is not nice to me, he or she is missing out—I'm a neat kid!"

- "If he or she doesn't want to be friends I won't die—I'll just try somebody else."

- _____

- _____

Say "Hi" and Tell Your Name

TRANSPARENCY #4

Ask a Question About . . .

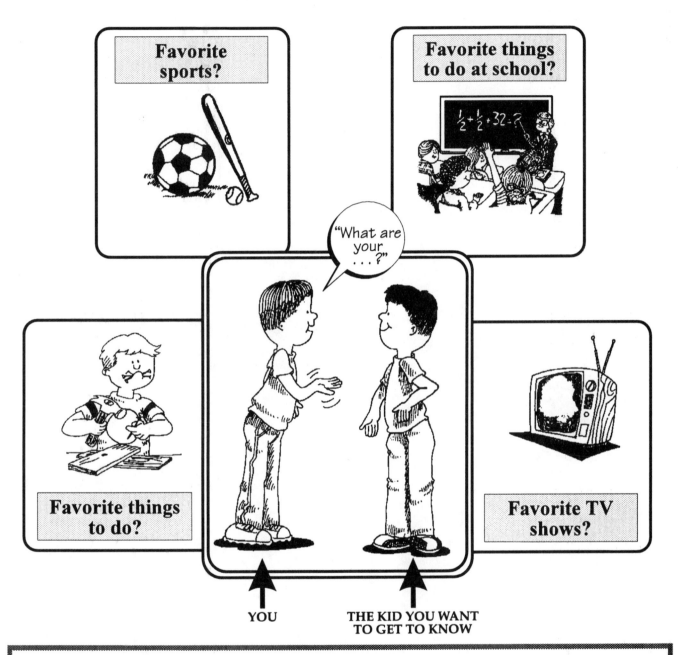

YOU   THE KID YOU WANT
TO GET TO KNOW

Your ideas:

How to Get Them Talking

"Yes" or "No" Questions	Questions That Get Them Talking
Closed questions: These usually start with words like "Do" or "Are."	*Open-ended questions: These usually start with words that begin with a "W" (e.g., "What" or "Where").*
Do you like our school?	
	What do you think of our school so far?
Are you on a soccer team?	
	What sports do you like?
Do you like to build models?	
	What do you like to do for fun?
Do you like to watch music videos?	
	What kind of music do you like?
Did you used to live around here?	
	Where else have you lived?

"Do you like soccer?"

"Yes."

"What sports do you like?"

"I like soccer, baseball, and I'm learning to ski."

TRANSPARENCY #6

Tell Something About Yourself

TRANSPARENCY #7

Suggest You Do Something Together

TRANSPARENCY #8A/HANDOUT #1A/POSTER #1A

1. **Relax and say encouraging things to yourself.**

    -   "I feel shy, but I can do it."

    -   "If it doesn't work out, I won't die."

2. **Say "Hi!" and tell them your name. (Smile!)**

3. **Ask a question:**

    -   "What's your name?"

    -   "Where do you live?"

    -   "Do you know any kids around here?"

    -   "Where do you go to school?"

    -   "Do you want to play something?"

    -   "Do you collect anything?"

    -   "Do you have any pets?"

    -   "What sports do you like?"

    -   "What games do you like to play?"

    -   "What TV shows do you like?"

How to Talk to Another Person (continued)

4. **Tell the other person something about yourself.**

- "I like that game, too."

- "I like to play basketball."

5. **Continue asking questions and telling something about yourself.**

- "Whose room are you in?"

- "I'm in Mrs. Smith's room."

- "What do you play at recess?"

- "I usually play soccer."

6. **Suggest that you do something together.**

- "Want to play on the bars?"

- "Want to sit together at lunch?"

"Want to play on my soccer team?"

"Sure!"

How to Make a New Friend

— STEP ONE —

(I think I'll take a chance and talk to that kid. I might make a friend.)

— STEP TWO —

(I'll say "Hi" and tell him my name.)

"Hi! I'm Toby. What's your name?"

"Hi! I'm Mark."

— STEP THREE —

(What do I do next? Oh, yeah—ask him something about himself.)

"I haven't seen you around before. Are you new here?"

"Yeah, I just moved here from Portland."

— STEP FOUR —

(Let's see . . . the next thing I do is tell him something about myself and ask him another question.)

"I moved here a couple of years ago. What sports do you like?"

"I like to play baseball."

— STEP FIVE —

(Now I tell him some more about me and ask more questions!)

"I like to play baseball, too—I especially like to pitch. What's your favorite position?"

"I like to play first base. I collect baseball cards of all my favorite players."

— STEP SIX —

(I like baseball cards, too. This kid could be fun. Before I go, I'll suggest we get together again.)

"Want to play catch with me next recess?"

"Yeah, that would be great!"

Starting a Conversation With Someone You Don't Know

Directions:

Write in the bubbles a conversation between these kids who don't know each other.

Starting a Conversation With Someone You Don't Know
(continued)

Directions:

Write in the bubbles a conversation between these kids who don't know each other.

When Trying to Make a New Friend Doesn't Work Out

Objective   Students will learn that not all efforts at making friends are rewarded by a new friendship.

Students will think of examples of positive self-talk to use in situations where their friendly overtures are not returned and choose between positive and negative courses of action.

Materials   Blank transparency and pen

Supplementary Activity #1 Handout, "When Trying to Make a New Friend Doesn't Work Out," for each student

Procedure   Tell the class that you want to read them a story about a girl just their age named Darlinda who had been learning about making friends with someone new. Tell them that Darlinda was confused because, even when she had followed all the steps, things hadn't worked out. Read the following story aloud:

> When Shannon joined her class in the middle of the year, Darlinda wondered what it would be like to be friends with her. Shannon was friendly and outgoing; she was good at reading and math and could draw anything! Darlinda admired her talent and thought it would be fun to have her for a friend.
>
> Darlinda tried for several weeks to make friends with Shannon. She smiled and asked her to sit by her at lunch. She offered to share her new colored markers and complimented Shannon's artwork. She did everything she had learned about how friends treat each other, but Shannon never really seemed to want to be friends with Darlinda. Shannon wasn't mean or rude; she just didn't seem to care if Darlinda was there or not.

Ask the class how they think Darlinda felt. Ask them to share experiences where they tried to make friends with someone and it hadn't worked out. Ask them what they did to try to establish the friendship, what the disappointing results were, and how they felt about it. Continue reading the story:

> Darlinda was feeling pretty blue. "I wonder why Shannon doesn't like me . . ." she thought. "Maybe she doesn't want to be my friend because I don't have as many clothes as some of the other girls. I bet she'd like me more if I wasn't such a loser!"

Ask the class what mistake they think Darlinda is making. Help students see that Darlinda has interpreted Shannon's lack of interest to mean that there's something wrong with Darlinda. Talk about the fact that there are some people we are drawn to and some we are not, even when there's nothing "wrong" with them or us.

Ask the class how Darlinda is hurting herself with her self-talk. Discuss the negative, self-deprecating quality of it. (You may wish to reread the last paragraph of the story.) Ask the class to help Darlinda think of things to say to herself to make herself feel better, such as:

- "Just because she doesn't want to be friends, doesn't mean there's something the matter with me."

- "I'll live, even if she doesn't want to be friends."

- "There are a lot of other people who want to be my friend even if she doesn't."

- "There are a lot of neat things about me, even if she can't see them."

- "She's missing out on a good friendship."

- "I don't need every single person to be my friend."

List these on a blank transparency.

Give students the Supplementary Activity #1 Handout and instruct them to help Darlinda decide what to do next. Tell them to cross out the thoughts they think would not be good choices. Have them choose one of the good choices and write why they think it would be a good choice on the lines at the bottom of the handout.

When Trying to Make a New Friend Doesn't Work Out

Darlinda has been trying to make friends with Shannon, but it hasn't worked out. Below are some of Darlinda's thoughts about what to do next.

- **Cross out** those thoughts that you think **would NOT be good choices** for her to take.

- **Pick one** of the remaining choices that you think **would be** a good solution to her problem. **Write** why you think this would work on the lines below.

I could look for someone else who might want a new friend.

I could buy Shannon a nice present.

I could hang around Shannon even more than I already do.

I could keep being friendly with Shannon, but spend more time with other girls.

I could tell the teacher that Shannon won't play with me.

I could ask Shannon why she thinks I'm not good enough to be her friend.

I could figure out what Shannon likes and try to be really good at that.

I could try to get the friends Shannon has now to be mad at her.

I could invite someone who wants to be my friend to come to my house on Saturday.

I could invite Shannon over to my house.

I could decide Shannon is stuck-up and start telling other kids what a loser she is.

_____

_____

_____

_____

The Getting to Know Someone Conversation Game

Objective   Students will practice asking open-ended questions to find out about a person they don't know by interviewing each other.

Materials   Supplementary Activity #2 Handout, "Getting-to-Know-Someone Conversation Form," for each student

Pencils

Transparency made from "Getting-to-Know-Someone Conversation Form" (Supplementary Activity #2 Transparency)

Procedure   Tell the class they are going to practice their conversation skills by interviewing their Learning Partners. Tell students that they will each be making up their character; they will choose a different name for themselves and decide where they lived before they moved here. Give them some suggestions to spur their creativity: Where do they live—in a house, apartment, mobile home, condo, on a farm or ranch, in a log cabin? Who do they live with—parent(s), aunt, uncle, grandmother, grandfather, brothers or sisters? What kind of pets do they have or did they have—dog, cat, horse, snake, parakeet, pig? Put the transparency on the overhead and go over the different topics, giving them a chance to think about them while they make up their character.

Remind the students about the question and answer skills they learned in the lesson—asking a question, listening to the answer, and then giving some information about themselves. Tell the Learning Partners to decide who will be the "Questioner." Questioners will ask their partner a question, write down the partner's answer, and then tell their partner some similar information about themselves. Their partner will write that information down on his or her own Getting-to-Know-Someone Conversation Form.

After the "getting-to-know-someone conversation" is completed, allow students to introduce their partners, using the information from their conversations.

In order to give the Learning Partners who didn't ask the questions a turn, have them exchange places with someone else who didn't ask questions. They will be the Questioner this time with their new Learning Partners. Distribute new Getting-to-Know-Someone Conversation Forms.

VARIATION

You may wish to have students working in triads, with one student acting as the "Observer." The Observer would notice if the questions were open-ended or "Yes" or "No" and whether the Questioner was smiling. Observers would give feedback at the end of each session, either to the pair or to the class. Triads would rotate roles.

Getting-to-Know-Someone Conversation Form

Questioner's Name _____

From _____

Other Person's Name _____

is from _____

lives _____

family _____

pets _____

interests and activities _____

_____

_____

_____

_____

likes _____

doesn't like _____

favorite food _____

favorite TV show _____

Tossing the Conversation Ball

Objective

Students will practice the six steps of having a conversation with someone they don't know by tossing a ball back and forth with another student who is role-playing a "new kid."

Materials

Tennis ball, Nerf™ ball, or paper wad for each pair of students

Posters #1A and #1B, "How to Talk to Another Person," from the lesson

Supplementary Activity #3 Handouts #1A and #1B, "New Kid Cards," cut apart, folded, and placed in sack or jar

Procedure

Students play in pairs seated across from each other. You may have two students or the whole class playing this game in pairs. Duplicate enough New Kid Cards so that there is at least one card for each pair playing; it doesn't matter if some pairs have duplicate cards.

Have partners designated as "New Kids" draw a New Kid Card to give them information about their character. (If you like, you may divide them according to probable sex so that no student draws a card that seems to be for the opposite sex.) The student designated as "Conversation Starter" acts out the first step, "Relax," and then smiles and introduces himself or herself. He or she then asks the first question, tossing the ball to the New Kid. The question should be an open-ended, rather than a "Yes or No" question. The New Kid answers the question, tossing the ball back to the Conversation Starter. The Conversation Starter tells something about himself or herself and then asks another question, tossing the ball to the New Kid.

Allow the question and answer period to continue for six or eight rounds, and then instruct the Conversation Starter to complete the last step, suggesting they get together another time.

Collect the New Kid Cards and reshuffle them. Partners change roles and the New Kids draw another New Kid Card. Students who draw the same card twice can draw a second time. (You may wish to add more New Kid Cards of your own or ask interested students to do so.)

New Kid Cards

You are the "new kid." You moved here three weeks ago from Hawaii. You are a very good swimmer and were learning to surfboard when your family moved away from Hawaii. You like the new school, but you can't get used to the cold winters here. Your cat just had kittens, but you had to give them all away before you moved.

You are the "new kid." You lived in a small town in Michigan before you moved here, and you loved to ski and snowmobile. The town you lived in was smaller than this one, and you find it strange that there are so many people who don't know each other. Your family is living in an apartment building while they're looking for a house. You have three hamsters and a golden retriever.

You are the "new kid." Your family moved here from Queens in New York City. Your mother is an artist, and you have drawn all your life. You can usually draw better than anyone in your class. Math is hard for you, but you like reading. You have a white fluffy cat and are a very good swimmer. Your mom is making you take piano lessons and you hate to practice.

You are the "new kid." You moved here from a ranch in West Texas. You grew up riding a horse and helping your uncle with the cattle. When your uncle died, you had to move here. The people are friendly here, but you miss your horse and old friends. You like the sports at this school and found out you're really good at baseball.

You are the "new kid." Your dad is in the military and has been stationed in Germany most of your life. You're having fun getting used to living in the United States. There are so many neat-looking clothes and lots of places to eat hamburgers and pizza! You've already made a couple of friends and think this is a friendly school.

You are the "new kid." You're visiting your dad for a month and would like to make a friend who enjoys swimming and listening to music. You like to go shopping and also play video games. You live with your mom in a big city a long way from here. No pets are allowed in your apartment, but you'd really like to have a dog.

New Kid Cards (continued)

You are the "new kid." This is your first time to go away to a summer camp, and most of the other kids seem to know each other. You love water sports and would like to find someone to be your canoe partner. You are a pretty good pitcher in softball, but you strike out more often than you get a hit. You have an iguana at home and really like to take nature hikes.

You are the "new kid." You used to go to a school not far from here, but your family just moved. Your parents are divorced and you live with your mom and step-father. You argue with him sometimes, but he helps you with your science homework and is pretty cool most of the time. You have a collection of old comic books and like to trade them with other kids. Your favorite foods are tacos and enchiladas. Your little sister has a yappy little dog that you hate.

You are the "new kid." You are what they would call "born to shop." In the town where you used to live, you lived in an apartment right across the street from a mall. You and your friends used to go over there on Saturday. This town is smaller and you haven't found anyone to do things with yet. Your mom is always bugging you to turn off the TV and do something else. But what is there to do? Homework? Yuk!

You are the "new kid." You just moved here last week from a town in California. You like to collect baseball cards and go to baseball card shows. You usually play baseball in the summer and are a pretty good hitter. You have a baseball signed by three of your favorite players. Baseball is your life!

You are the "new kid." You just moved here from Mexico City and think this is a neat town, even though it's not as big as Mexico City is. One of the things you like best here is the music, even though your mom won't let you go to any concerts until you're a teenager. You also really like to go to the movies. There are several you'd like to see right now. You have a kitten that wandered up to your door. It was hungry so you fed it and gave it a home.

How Other Kids Make a New Friend

Directions:

The following are real suggestions made by students like you about how to make a friend. Read them and underline the ideas you like most, then answer the "Dear Abby" letter at the end, giving what you think would be the best advice.

Other Kids' Ideas on How to Make a Friend

"The first thing to do to someone you want to be friends with is to smile. This shows them that you are interested in making friends with them. If they smile back, tell them your name and start a conversation."

—Sherry

"To make a friend you have to be willing to talk first. Introduce yourself and find out their name. Then ask them about their hobbies and interests."

—Jorden

"I make friends by being nice. For instance, in P.E. we were practicing serves in volleyball and I handed the ball to this girl once in a while so she could have more turns. That's how we became friends."

—Darla

"When I want to make a friend there are two things I try to do: be nice and be funny. Being nice is the most important, but being funny helps, too, because kids like to laugh. So b funny, but don't use put-downs. They're not funny."

—Bart

"I usually make friends by talking to others and saying something friendly. For instance, if I'm playing basketball at recess with a guy I want to be friends with, I say 'Nice pass!' or 'Good shot!' Soon we're talking about more than sports and we're hanging out together."

—Darren

"A good way I've found to make a friend is to walk up to somebody who looks a little lonely and introduce myself. Another way is to defend somebody who is being bullied."

—Chuck

(continued)

"I like to ask questions to see if we have anything in common. If we do, I say something like, 'Maybe we can do something together sometime.'"

—*Kuniko*

"I say 'How's it going?' to strike up a conversation. A few days later I ask them if they want to sit by me at lunch. I try and do this with people I'm pretty sure I won't get turned down by, otherwise I'd just end up getting hurt."

—*Rick*

"The way I make friends is to try to notice the kids who smile at me or talk to me. Then I ask them if they'd like to work on a school project with me or come to my house."

—*Tracy*

Dear Abby:

I have just moved to a new school and have not made any friends yet. There is one group at school that seems really neat and just the kind of kids I want to be friends with. There are a couple of kids in particular I'd like to get to know. I would feel dumb just asking them if I could join them. Do you know of some ways I could get into this group without being embarrassed?

Signed,
Want To Belong

Dear "Want To Belong,"

Yours truly,
Abby

What's one thing you would <u>never</u> do if you wanted to make a friend?

A p p e n d i x   A

Using Literature to Enhance Students' Understanding of Friendship

The following lists of children's books all relate to friendship themes and were generated in the following manner:

A master list was compiled utilizing the latest edition of *Bookfinder* and the *Anthology of Children's Picture Books*. This list was divided into a compilation appropriate for grades K-3. (A compilation for grades 4-6 can be found in *Teaching Friendship Skills: Intermediate Version*.) This list was sent to librarians in public libraries, public schools, and at children's book stores. The librarians were asked to comment on age appropriateness, readability, and popularity of the books with children. They also selected their own favorites. The lists on the following pages are the result. You can readily promote students' understanding of friendship issues through books either by reading aloud to the class or by encouraging independent reading.

When you read aloud to your class you'll find many opportunities for discussing how a character felt about something or why the character made particular decisions. You can ask a number of questions requiring students to use critical thinking skills. These discussions can strengthen students' friendship skills and increase their understanding of others.

A useful technique is to stop reading a story just short of the conclusion and ask the class to end the story. You can compare their conclusion with the author's.

These books can be used as an introduction to a friendship lesson or to extend a theme a lesson presents. They can be placed in a "Friendship Center" and used for independent reading. They can be given to parents to read to children at home. Students can reconstruct favorite stories through art and drama. They can use them as springboards for writing their own friendship stories.

By reading about the frienships of others, students can become better equipped to understand social relationships of their own.

Books for Kindergarten and First Grade

The following list of books would work well for reading aloud to kindergarten and first grade students. In addition, some first grade students and most second grade students could read these books themselves. The books that are starred are librarians' and children's favorites.

Anglund, J.W.		*A Friend Is Someone Who Likes You*
Ardizzone, E.		*Tim and Lucy Go to Sea*
Baker, B.	☆	*Digby and Kate*
Bare, C.		*Guinea Pigs Don't Read Books*
Beim, L.	☆	*Two Is a Team*
Brandenberg, F.	☆	*A Friend Can Help*
	☆	*Leo and Emily*
	☆	*Nice New Neighbors*
Briggs, R.	☆	*The Snowman*
Burningham, J.		*Aldo*
		The Friend
Carle, E.		*Do You Want to Be My Friend?*
Clifton, L.		*Everett Anderson's Friend*
Cohen, M.	☆	*Best Friends*
	☆	*Will I Have a Friend?*
Crary, E.		*I Want to Play*
		I Want It
		I Can't Wait
Dabcovich, L.	☆	*Mrs. Huggins and Her Hen Hannah*
De Beer, H.		*Little Polar Bear*
Delton, J.		*Two Good Friends*
		Rabbit Finds a Way
		Two is Company
De Paola, T.		*Oliver Button is a Sissy*
De Regniers, B.S.		*May I Bring a Friend?*
Elliottare, D.		*Grover Goes to School*
Erickson, R.		*Toad for Tuesday*
		Warton and Mortan

Fujikawa, G. . . . . *Welcome Is a Wonderful Word*

. . . . *That's Not Fair*

. . . . *Jenny Learns a Lesson*

Heine, H. . . . . ☆ *Friends*

Hoban, R. . . . . ☆ *A Bargain for Frances*

. . . . *Best Friends for Frances*

Hughes, S. . . . . ☆ *Moving Molly*

Komiako, L. . . . . ☆ *Annie Bananie*

Krasilovsky, P. . . . . ☆ *The Shy Little Girl*

Lionni, L. . . . . *It's Mine*

. . . . *Little Blue and Little Yellow*

. . . . ☆ *Alexander and the Wind-Up Mouse*

Lobel, A. . . . . *Days with Frog and Toad*

. . . . *Frog and Toad All Year*

. . . . ☆ *Frog and Toad are Friends*

. . . . ☆ *Frog and Toad Together*

Lystad, M.H. . . . . *That New Boy*

Majewski, J. . . . . *A Friend For Oscar Mouse*

Marshall, E. . . . . *Three by the Sea*

. . . . *Fox and His Friends*

Marshall, J. . . . . ☆ *George and Martha*

. . . . *George and Martha Encore*

. . . . *George and Martha One Fine Day*

. . . . *George and Martha Rise and Shine*

Miller, E. . . . . ☆ *Mousekin Finds a Friend*

Minarik, E.H. . . . . *Little Bear's Friend*

Newberry, C.T. . . . . ☆ *Marshmallow*

Oxenbury, H. . . . . ☆ *Friends*

Robins, J. . . . . ☆ *Addie Meets Max*

Rogers, F. . . . . ☆ *Making Friends*

. . . . *Moving*

Ross, P. . . . . ☆ *Meet M and M*

Seuling, B. . . . . *The Great Big Elephant and the Very Small Elephant*

Sharmot, M.W. . . . . ☆ *Gladys Told Me to Meet Her Here*

. . . . ☆ *I'm Not Oscar's Friend Anymore*

. . . . ☆ *Mitchell is Moving*

Sherman, I.	☆	*I Do Not Like It When My Friend Comes To Visit*
Steig, W.	☆	*Amos and Boris*
Stevenson, J.	☆	*Fast Friends*
Tsutsui, Y.	☆	*Anna's Secret Friend*
Udry, J.M.	☆	*Let's Be Enemies*
Vincent, G.		*Breakfast Time, Ernest and Celestine*
	☆	*Where Are You, Ernest and Celestine?*
Waber, B.		*Ira Sleeps Over*
Wells, R.		*Timothy Goes to School*
Wiethorn, R.		*Rock Finds a Friend*
Wildsmith, B.	☆	*The Lazy Bear*

An Annotated List of Books to Read to Kindergarten and First Graders

☆ *Frog and Toad are Friends*, *Frog and Toad Together*, and *Frog and Toad All Year*, by Arnold Lobel, are about two friends who always help each other. They could be read by some first and most second graders.

☆ *Timothy Goes to School*, by Rosemary Wells, *Will I Have A Friend?*, by Miriam Cohen, and *Grover Goes to School*, by Dan Elliottare, are good books to read to K-1 students when the school year begins.

☆ *Best Friends for Frances*, by Russell Hoban, is a fun story about boy-girl and sibling friendships.

☆ *Little Bear's Friend*, by E.H. Minarik; kindergarteners love this story about a little girl and a bear.

☆ *Do You Want to be My Friend?*, by Eric Carle, is a picture book with no words about a mouse seeking friendship. You can show it to K-1 students and have them make up the story.

☆ *The Hating Book*, by Charlotte Zolotow, is a story about a misunderstanding between two best friends. It's great for K-2 students.

☆ *Best Friends*, by Miriam Cohen, is about how best friends make up after a fight.

☆ *We Are Best Friends*, by Aliki, and *Janey*, by Charlotte Zolotow, are stories which tell how new friendships can be made and old friendships kept. Students who have had a best friend move away will love these stories.

☆ *Amos and Boris*, by William Stieg, is a sensitive story of a whale and a mouse, and tells how each learns to appreciate and respect the other's uniqueness.

☆ *Two Good Friends*, by Judy Delton, tells the story of Duck and Bear, two friends who were very different from each other. They learn to resolve their conflicts and to compliment one another.

Books for Kindergarten Through Third Grade

The following books are great for reading aloud to kindergarten through third grade students. In addition, some second grade and most third grade students could read these books themselves. The books that are starred are librarians' and children's favorites.

Aliki	☆ *Overnight at Mary Bloom's*
	☆ *We Are Best Friends*
Anglund, J.W.	*A Friend is Somebody Who Likes You*
Asch, F.	*Oats and Wild Apples*
Brown, P.	*Hickory*
Carlson, N.	*Marie, Louise, and Christopher*
Cohen, M.	*First Grade Takes A Test*
Craig, H.	☆ *The Night of the Paper Bag*
Delacre, L.	*Nathan's Fishing Trip*
Delaney, N.	*Bert and Barney*
Fleischman, S.	*The Scarebird*
Graham, B.	☆ *Crusher is Coming*
Henkes, K.	*Chester's Way*
	Jessica
Hoban, R.	☆ *Best Friends for Frances*
Hoff, S.	*Who Will be My Friends?*
Holabird, K.	*Angelina and Alice*
Keats, E.J.	☆ *A Letter to Amy*
	Apartment Three
Keller, H.	☆ *Lizzie's Invitation*
Kellogg, S.	*Won't Somebody Play With Me?*
Kessler, L.	*Here Comes the Strikeout*
King, L.L.	*Because of Lozo Brown*
Kissey, J.	*Old Bear*
Komiako, L.	*Earl's Too Cool for Me*
Krauss, R.	*I'll Be You and You Be Me*
Lester, H.	*The Wizard, the Fairy and the Magic Chicken*
Marshall, J.	☆ *What's the Matter with Carruthers?*

Stevenson, J. . . . . ☆ *No Friends*

. . . . *The Worst Person in the World*

. . . . *The Worst Person in the World at Crab Beach*

Turkle, B. . . . . *Thy Friend, Obadiah*

Viorst, J. . . . . ☆ *Rosie and Michael*

Waber, B. . . . . *Ira Says Goodbye*

. . . . ☆ *Ira Sleeps Over*

. . . . ☆ *Loveable Lyle*

. . . . ☆ *Nobody is Perfick*

Weiss, N. . . . . ☆ *Maude and Sally*

White, E.B. . . . . ☆ *Charlotte's Web*

Whittman, S. . . . . *A Special Trade*

Williams, V.B. . . . . *Stringbean's Trip to the Shining Sea*

Winthrop, E. . . . . *Katharine's Doll*

. . . . ☆ *Lizzie and Harold*

Yeoman, J. . . . . *Mouse Trouble*

Zolotow, C. . . . . ☆ *The New Friend*

. . . . ☆ *The Hating Book*

. . . . *It's Not Fair*

. . . . ☆ *Janey*

. . . . ☆ *The Quarreling Book*

. . . . *My Friend John*

. . . . ☆ *The White Marble*

Topic Bibliography for Primary Age Students

Books About MAKING NEW FRIENDS:

Aliki . . . . *We Are Best Friends*

Anglund, J.W. . . . . *A Friend Is Someone Who Likes You*

Barkin, J. . . . . *Are We Still Friends?*

Belpre, P. . . . . *Santiago*

Bograd, L. . . . . *Lost in the Store*

Cameron, A. . . . . *The Stories Julian Tells*

Carrick, M. . . . . *Tramp*

Cleary, B.B. . . . . *Henry and the Paper Route*

Cohen, M.	*Will I Have A Friend?*
Coombs, P.	*Lisa and the Grompet*
Crary, E.	*I Want To Play*
DeRegniers, B.S.	*How Joe and Sam the Moose got Together*
Hariss, D.J.	*The School Mouse*
Hickman, M.W.	*My Friend William Moved Away*
Horvath, B.	*Be Nice to Josephine*
Hurwitz, J.	*Aldo Applesauce*
Iwasaki, C.	*Will You Be My Friend?*
Jacobsen, J.	*City Sing for Me: A Country Child Moves to the City*
Jewell, N.	*Bus Ride*
Keats, E.J.	*Apartment Three*
Kellogg, S.	*A Rose for Pinkerton*
Krasilovsky, P.	*The Shy Little Girl*
	Susan Sometimes
Kroll, S.	*The Tyrannosaurus Game*
Lysatd, M.	*That New Boy*
Margolis, R.	*Wish Again, Big Bear*
McGovern, A.	*Scram, Kid*
Miles, B.	*Having a Friend*
Minarik, E.H.	*Little Bear's Friend*
Moncure, J.B.	*A New Boy in Kindergarten*
Montgomery, E.R.	*The Mystery of the Boy Next Door*
Pearson, S.	*Molly Moves Out*
Perrine, M.	*Nannabah's Friend*
Prather, R.	*New Neighbors*
Priceman, M.	*Friend or Frog*
Rinkoff, B.J.	*Rutherford, T. Finds 21B*
Robinat, H.G.	*Jay and the Marigold*
Robinson, N.K.	*Wendy and the Bullies*
Schick, E.	*5A and 7B*
Schultz, G.	*The Blue Valentine*
Stevenson, J.	*Fast Friends*
Udry, J.M.	*What Mary Jo Shared*
Van Leeuwen, J.	*Timothy's Flower*
Vogel, I.-M.	*Hello, Henry*

Wiethorne, R.J. . . . . *Rock Finds a Friend*

Wiseman, B. . . . . *Moris and Boris*

Zolotow, C. . . . . *New Friend*

. . . . *A Tiger Called Thomas*

Books About BEST FRIENDS:

Barkin, C. & James, E. . . . . *Are We Still Best Friends?*

Behrens, J.Y. . . . . *Together*

Bradenberg, A.L. . . . . *We Are Best Friends*

Brown, M.B. . . . . *Best Friends*

Burningham, J.M. . . . . *The Friend*

Delton, J. . . . . *Lee Henry's Best Friend*

. . . . *Two Is Company*

Gantos, J. . . . . *Fair Weather Friends*

Gordon, S. . . . . *Crystal is the New Girl*

Haas, D. . . . . *Poppy and the Outdoors Cat*

Hoban, R.C. . . . . *Best Friends for Frances*

Ichikawa, S. . . . . *Friends*

Madison, W. . . . . *Marinka, Katinka and Me*

Marshall, J. . . . . *George and Martha Rise and Shine*

Myers, B. . . . . *Not At Home?*

Seuling, B. . . . . *The Great Big Elephant and the Very
  Small Elephant*

Sharmat, M.W. . . . . *Burton and Dudley*

. . . . *Gladys Told Me to Meet Her Here*

. . . . *Mitchell Is Moving*

Vigna, J. . . . . *The Hiding House*

Wittman, S. . . . . *Pelly and Peak*

Zelonky, J. . . . . *My Best Friend Moved Away*

Zolotow, C.S. . . . . *It's Not Fair*

. . . . *The White Marble*

Books About KEEPING FRIENDS:

Brown, M.B. . . . . *Best Friends*

Gauch, P.L. . . . . *Christina Katerina & the Box*

Hopkins L.B. . . . . *I Loved Rose Ann*

Panek, D. . . . . *Matilda Hippo Has a Big Mouth*

Sharmat, M.W. . . . . *Lucretia the Unbearable*

Stolz, M.S. . . . . *Maximilian's World*

Books About LACK OF FRIENDS:

Snyder, Z.K. . . . . *Come On, Patsy*

Books About THE MEANING OF FRIENDSHIP:

Annett, C. . . . . *When the Porcupine Moved In*

Berger, T. . . . . *Being Alone, Being Together*

Burton, V.L. . . . . *Mike Mulligan and His Steam Shovel*

Charlip, R. & Supree, B. . . . . *Harlequin and the Gift of Many Colors*

Clifton, L. . . . . *Three Wishes*

Delton, J. . . . . *Two Good Friends*

Freeman, D. . . . . *Corduroy*

Goffstein, M.B. . . . . *Goldie the Dollmaker*

Hogan, P. . . . . *I Hate Boys, I Hate Girls*

. . . . *Sometimes I Get So Mad*

Holly, A.H. . . . . *Small Bear Builds A Playhouse*

Lexau, J.M. . . . . *I'll Tell On You*

Thomas, I. . . . . *Hi, Mrs. Mallory!*

Turkle, B. . . . . *Thy Friend, Obadiah*

Wittman, S.A. . . . . *The Wonderful Mrs. Trumbly*

A p p e n d i x   B

Friendship Games

Use the following games to reinforce the concepts and skills taught in the lessons:

- "The Helps or Hurts Game"
- "The Warm Fuzzy Game" (Lesson 7, Supplementary Activity #4)

The Helps or Hurts Game

Objective   Students will identify positive and negative friendship behaviors.

Materials   Master List of Statements (The Helps or Hurts Game—Master Lists
           of Statements #1A and #1B)

           The Helps or Hurts Game Cards 1-16 (The Helps or Hurts
           Game—Game Cards)

           Helps or Hurts Squares run off on pink (or pastel) paper and gray (or
           dark) paper

           Small envelopes

           Larger envelope or small bag

           Transparency masters (optional) (The Helps or Hurts Game—Master
           Lists of Statements #1A and #1B)

Procedure   This game is similar to tic-tac-toe. Students win by getting three pink
           "things that HELP friendships" squares (Helps Squares) in a row.

           Before play begins, make copies of the Game Cards. Cut the pages in
           two so that you have one Game Card for each student (there are 16
           different cards). Next, make copies of the Helps and Hurts Squares,
           copying Helps onto pink paper and Hurts onto gray. Cut these and place
           ten Helps Squares and ten Hurts Squares into each of the small
           envelopes. Last, cut up the master list of Helps or Hurts Statements,
           and place all of these into the larger envelope or bag. Two blank boxes
           are included for you to fill in statements relevant to your classroom.

           To play, give each student a game card and one of the small envelopes
           containing the Helps and Hurts Squares. Now, begin drawing Helps or
           Hurts Statements from your large envelope and reading these aloud to
           the class. (For younger students, you can make transparencies of the
           Master List of Statements, cut these out and, as you draw them, place
           them one at a time on an overhead projector so all the students can see
           them.)

           For each statement you draw, ask your students: "Does this help or does
           this hurt a friendship?" If it "helps," have them place a pink Helps
           Square over that statement on their Game Card. If it "hurts," have them

place a gray Hurts Square there. Not all students will have each statement on their individual game card.

When a player has three Helps Squares in a row (horizontally, vertically, or diagonally), he or she calls out "Friend!" Then that student reads back the three things that help friendships which they covered on their card. The student can then receive a small reward such as a star, gummy bear, or something from your own classroom reward system. (Three Hurts Squares in a row do NOT count as a win, because only helpful things win friendships.)

You may also play blackout, i.e., until all of the players' squares are covered on a Game Card.

Pokes you	Copies your answers	Teases you
Is bossy	Takes your things	Saves you a place
Cuts in front of you	Cheats at games	Helps you
Makes fun of you	Ignores you	Invites you over
Tells your secrets	Compliments you	Tattles on you

THE HELPS OR HURTS GAME—MASTER LIST OF STATEMENTS #1B

Encourages you	Plays fair	Shares with you
Listens to you	Remembers your birthday	Calls you names
Lets you go first	Apologizes	Plays with you
Helps you with schoolwork	Gives you a hug	Lies to you
Trips you		

THE HELPS OR HURTS GAME—GAME CARDS

Game Card 1

Plays fair	Plays with you	Calls you names
Shares with you	Is bossy	Helps you
Compliments you	Tattles on you	Saves you a place

Game Card 2

Apologizes	Plays fair	Compliments you
Shares with you	Copies your answers	Makes fun of you
Pokes you	Helps you	Remembers your birthday

THE HELPS OR HURTS GAME—GAME CARDS (continued)

Game Card 3

Tells your secrets	Listens to you	Plays fair
Trips you	Makes fun of you	Encourages you
Cheats at games	Calls you names	Apologizes

Game Card 4

Calls you names	Plays with you	Pokes you
Plays fair	Shares with you	Gives you a hug
Compliments you	Ignores you	Saves you a place

Game Card 5

Plays with you	Gives you a hug	Apoligizes
Plays fair	Shares with you	Ignores you
Calls you names	Lies to you	Listens to you

Game Card 6

Compliments you	Takes your things	Plays fair
Encourages you	Shares with you	Tattles on you
Calls you names	Plays with you	Remembers your birthday

Game Card 7

Cuts in front of you	Shares with you	Helps you with schoolwork
Lets you go first	Lies to you	Listens to you
Plays fair	Calls you names	Compliments you

Game Card 8

Apologizes	Copies your answers	Plays with you
Helps you	Teases you	Shares with you
Calls you names	Trips you	Gives you a hug

THE HELPS OR HURTS GAME—GAME CARDS (continued)

Game Card 9

Plays fair	Helps you	Tattles on you
Lets you go first	Is bossy	Apologizes
Encourages you	Plays with you	Copies your answers

Game Card 10

Remembers your birthday	Lies to you	Apologizes
Compliments you	Teases you	Listens to you
Takes your things	Trips you	Invites you over

THE HELPS OR HURTS GAME—GAME CARDS (continued)

Game Card 11

Lies to you	Plays fair	Pokes you
Saves you a place	Tells your secrets	Remembers your birthday
Compliments you	Helps you	Listens to you

Game Card 12

Lets you go first	Pokes you	Plays fair
Gives you a hug	Saves you a place	Makes fun of you
Copies your answers	Helps you with schoolwork	Shares with you

THE HELPS OR HURTS GAME—GAME CARDS (continued)

Game Card 13

Tells your secrets	Helps you with schoolwork	Gives you a hug
Shares with you	Helps you	Cuts in front of you
Compliments you	Is bossy	Remembers your birthday

Game Card 14

Cheats at games	Trips you	Teases you
Apologizes	Pokes you	Shares with you
Plays with you	Saves you a place	Tells you a secret

THE HELPS OR HURTS GAME—GAME CARDS (continued)

Game Card 15

Encourages you	Takes your things	Apologizes
Helps you with schoolwork	Compliments you	Cheats at games
Makes fun of you	Plays with you	Invites you over

Game Card 16

Compliments you	Gives you a hug	Cuts in front of you
Tells your secrets	Invites you over	Helps you
Apologizes	Ignores you	Plays fair

HELPS OR HURTS SQUARES

A p p e n d i x   C

School-Wide Procedures That Promote Friendship

Friendship Weeks

At the beginning of "Friendship Weeks," a set of posters which name the keys to friendship can be put in each teacher's mailbox. The posters are contained in Appendix D. These look best when run off on different colors. Teachers can be asked to display one poster each day in a prominent place in the classroom. The messages on these posters can be read over the intercom by the principal or school counselor. The posters serve as visual reminders throughout the day of the friendship behavior students should focus on.

Friendship Awards Assembly

This activity is a good culmination to the school-wide Friendship Weeks. Each teacher can be given the set of awards that follow (Awards #1-#8) and can designate students who exemplify the quality specified on each award. The teacher can fill out the awards and sign them. School principals or counselors can be asked to sign them as well.

It is best to have separate "Friendship Awards Assemblies" for primary and intermediate students due to the length of the assembly. During the assembly, each teacher can present the awards to his or her students.

During the "Friendship Awards Assembly," different students can present things they have written or produced as a result of doing one of the many activities in this manual.

Friendship Tickets

This activity is a school-wide "Friendship Raffle." It is a fun accompaniment to Friendship Weeks. Make copies of the Friendship Tickets handout (behind the Friendship Awards) and cut these into tickets. Make a Raffle Box for each classroom by decorating a small box or coffee can. Cut a hole in the lid large enough for the tickets to be inserted. Make a larger Raffle Box for the office.

Explain to students over the school intercom that during the next few weeks everyone in the school will be participating in a Friendship Raffle. When anyone does something particularly friendly or helps another person in some way, the recipient of the friendly behavior can fill out a "Friendship Ticket" as a thank you to that person. All school staff members including lunchroom, playground, and custodial staff can also be asked to be on the lookout for friendly behaviors they see students do and can write up tickets for these students as well.

Friendship Tickets can first be put into the Raffle Box in each classroom. At the end of each day, a student can transfer these tickets to the large Raffle Box in the office. At the beginning or end of each day or at the end of the week, three or four tickets should be drawn from the raffle box and winning students should receive a designated prize or privilege. The winners' names and the friendly behavior they did should be read over the intercom.

FRIENDSHIP
TICKET

Their Name _____ Grade _____

Your Name _____

What they did: _____

_____

_____

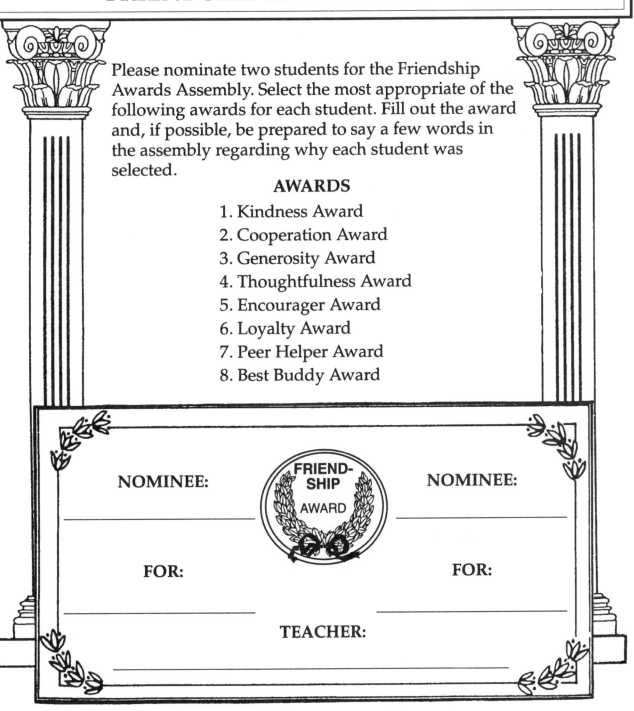

TEACHER NOMINATION FORM
FOR
FRIENDSHIP AWARDS ASSEMBLY

Please nominate two students for the Friendship Awards Assembly. Select the most appropriate of the following awards for each student. Fill out the award and, if possible, be prepared to say a few words in the assembly regarding why each student was selected.

AWARDS

1. Kindness Award
2. Cooperation Award
3. Generosity Award
4. Thoughtfulness Award
5. Encourager Award
6. Loyalty Award
7. Peer Helper Award
8. Best Buddy Award

NOMINEE: _____   NOMINEE: _____

FRIEND-SHIP AWARD

FOR: _____   FOR: _____

TEACHER: _____

1.

2.

3.

4.

5.

6.

7.

8.

To all who may read this document:

is hereby officially honored
for outstanding kindness to others.

Teacher

Date

Award for
Kindness

FRIEND-
SHIP
AWARD

—Award for—

Cooperation

FRIEND-SHIP AWARD

To all who may read this document:

_____

is hereby officially honored for outstanding performance in cooperating with others.

_____ _____
Teacher   *Date*

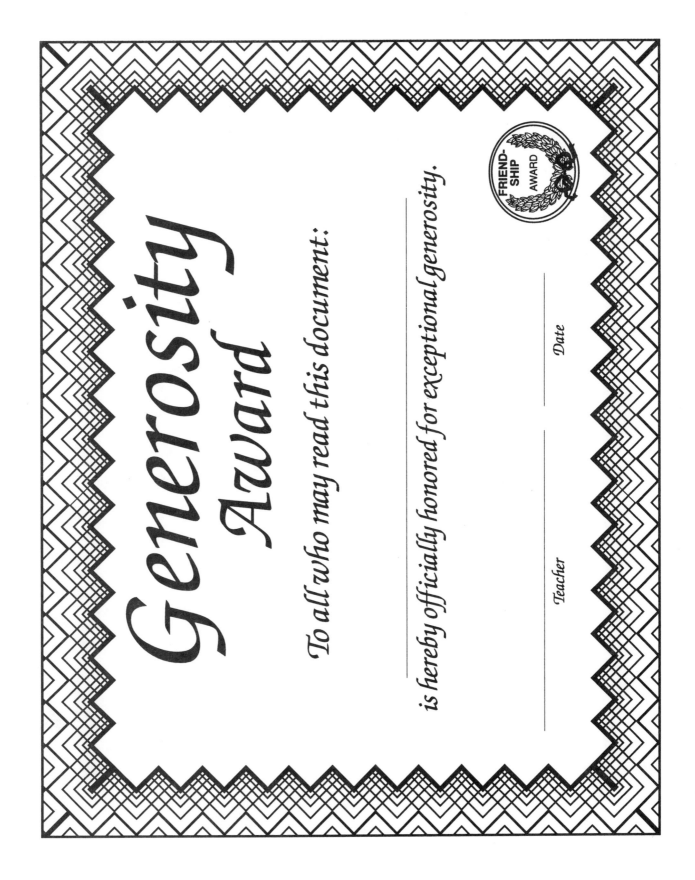

Generosity
Award

To all who may read this document:

is hereby officially honored for exceptional generosity.

FRIEND-
SHIP
AWARD

Teacher

Date

—*Award for*—

Thoughtfulness

To all who may read this document:

_____

*is hereby officially honored
for outstanding thoughtfulness.*

_____   _____
Teacher   *Date*

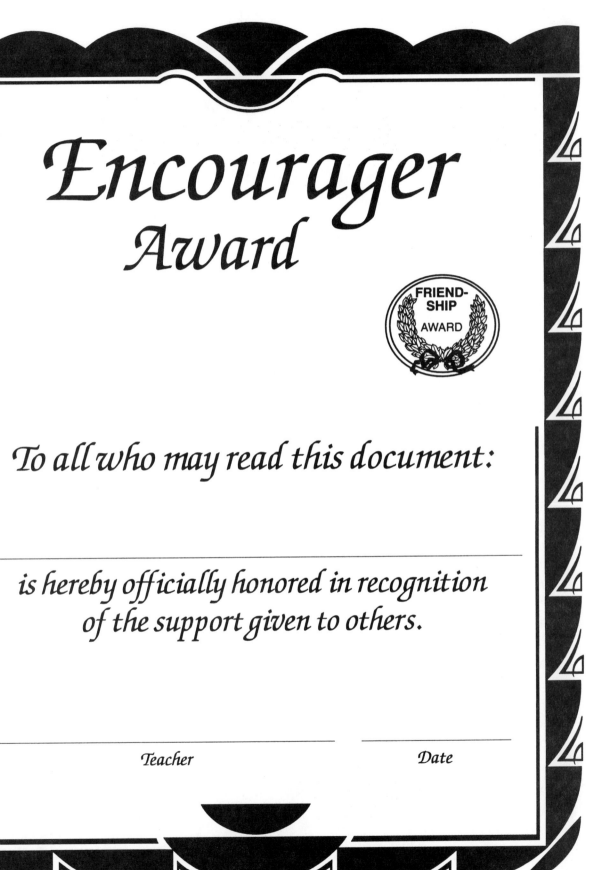

Encourager
Award

To all who may read this document:

_____

is hereby officially honored in recognition
of the support given to others.

_____   _____
Teacher   Date

Loyalty

Award

To all who may read this document:

is hereby officially honored in recognition of outstanding loyalty to others.

Date

Teacher

FRIEND-SHIP AWARD

Peer Helper Award

FRIEND-
SHIP

AWARD

To all who may read this document:

_____

is hereby officially honored in recognition
of reaching out to help a friend.

_____   _____
Teacher   Date

—Award for—
Best Buddy

To all who may read this document:

_____

*is hereby officially honored in recognition
of being a good friend to others.*

_____   _____
Teacher   *Date*

FRIENDSHIP TICKETS

FRIENDSHIP
TICKET

Grade _____

Their Name _____
Your Name _____
What they did: _____

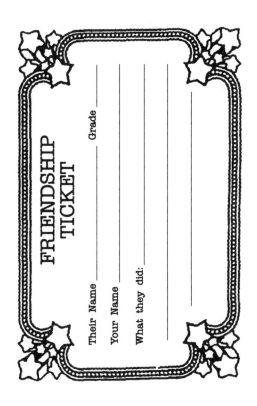

FRIENDSHIP
TICKET

Grade _____

Their Name _____
Your Name _____
What they did: _____

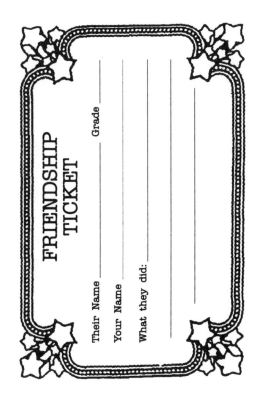

FRIENDSHIP
TICKET

Grade _____

Their Name _____
Your Name _____
What they did: _____

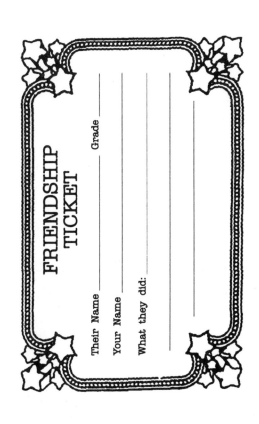

FRIENDSHIP
TICKET

Grade _____

Their Name _____
Your Name _____
What they did: _____

A p p e n d i x   D

Posters

1.	Treat others the way you want to be treated.
2.	Make others feel special.
3.	Offer to share things with others.
4.	Tell others what you like about them.
5.	When someone has been successful—compliment them.
6.	Be honest with others.
7.	Try to make others feel better when they make mistakes.
8.	Apologize if you hurt another's feelings.
9.	Apologizing doesn't always mean you were wrong—it means you're sorry.
10.	Don't give put-downs.
11.	Look for the good in a person when you feel like saying something mean.
12.	Let your friends have other friends.

Treat others the way you want to be treated.

Make others feel special.

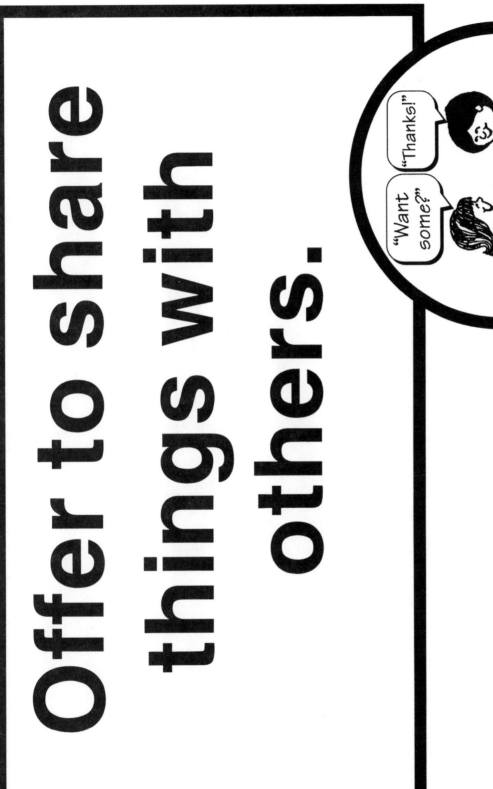

Tell others what you like about them.

"You're generous!"

When someone has been successful—compliment them.

POSTER #6

Be honest with others.

Try to make others feel better when they make mistakes.

POSTER #8

Apologize if you hurt another's feelings.

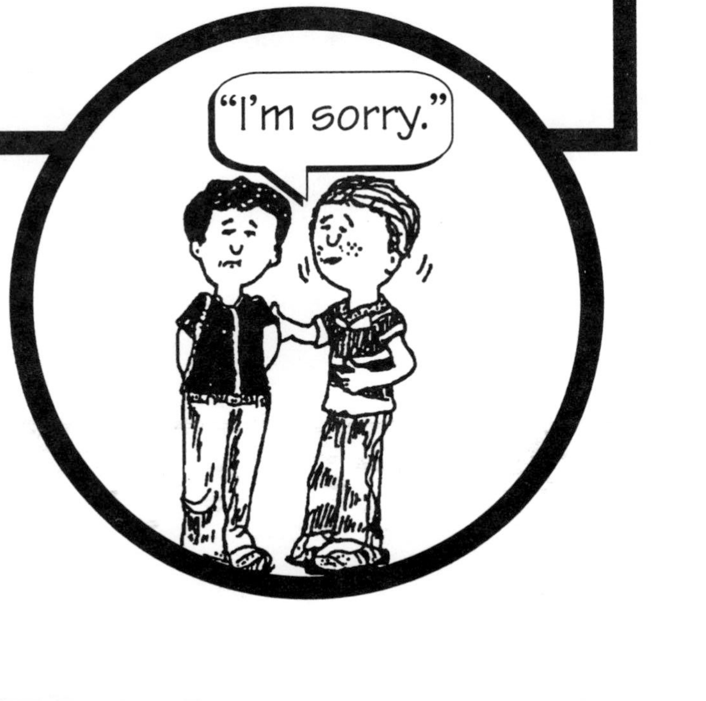

POSTER #9

Apologizing doesn't always mean you were wrong—it means you're sorry.

"I'm sorry."

Don't give put-downs.

POSTER #11

Look for the good in a person when you feel like saying somethign mean.

Let your friends have other friends.